PRAISE  *RED*

"Elictia has done an incredible job of weaving her stories from her years in front of the camera seamlessly with the Christian values that guide her life. We grew up together, working, learning, climbing the ladder of the broadcasting world and sharing the intoxicating highs and the heartbreaking lows that this business serves up on a regular basis. I was surprised when Elictia left television for good, I always thought she would come back, she was that good. But now I understand that she has redefined her life's purpose and this book can help you redefine yours."

—Kevin Frazier, cohost, *Entertainment Tonight*

"I was highly impressed with Elictia during our first interview/meeting many years ago. I truly believed, back then, that with a balance of support and guidance she was going to be extremely successful in life. Elictia has an incredible gift of communicating both in person and on paper. This gift is clearly seen in her book, *Redefining Red*. Elictia's ability to help others build positive self-esteem, believe in themselves, and follow their dreams is very evident throughout the pages. I believe potential readers will benefit from picking up this great book!"

—Roy Hamilton, former FOX Sports, Senior
Vice -President, Talent and Development

"This morning I began reading Pastor Elictia's book *Redefining Red*. My intention was to briefly scan it in order to write a recommendation. Instead, I got hijacked by the Holy Spirit! Like Ruth, 'I *happened* upon the field belonging to Boaz.' Like Jacob, I lighted upon a certain place, that happened to be 'the gate of heaven.' This book spoke deeply to me in my own personal journey. It is my hope that it will do the same for everyone who reads it."

—Bishop Joseph L. Garlington, Sr., founding pastor, Covenant
Church of Pittsburgh; presiding bishop, Reconciliation!
an international network of churches and ministries

"This beautifully written book's practical wisdom, drawn from Elictia's personal experience as well as from the experience of Bible characters, makes this a treasure to read and embrace. Elictia has written truth that is simple to understand, yet remarkably powerful enough to transform our approach to life's experiences. *Redefining Red* shows us how 'our red moments can become green lights for trusting God and embracing our divine destiny,' proving that red truly is the new green!"

—Drs. Andre and Jenny Roebert, founders and
co-presidents, Faith Broadcasting Network

"Pastor Elictia Hart has the ability to be a straight shooter (prophetic), yet compassionate (pastoral), and in her new book *Redefining Red*, her way with words (preacher) brings a message that is needed by so many today! Her love for people, the church, and God shine through page to page! This book will not only encourage and inspire you but will take each reader to another level in life. Jesus said go, and Elictia agrees. We are to be people of action, turning every negative into a positive. A great read!"

—Peter Mortlock ThD, senior pastor,
City Impact Churches, New Zealand

"Pastor Elictia Hart turns the light on to what the true color of God's plan is for our lives. In the culture we live in, the 'political correctness' of our times has overshadowed the purity of the Word of God, but Elictia gets it right. The new normal is red. The Blood, the Cross, His power and authority. Be emboldened by this timely book and get ready to accelerate. The red means GO!!"

—Judy Jacobs, worship leader, copastor, author

"Special people usually produce special products and Elictia is in a unique category of special people. The top 1 percent of successful people in the world are there because of discipline, commitment, passion, knowledge and creativity. As a public figure, speaker, and author, Elictia has earned her place to guide, direct, mentor, and develop people. Her book is not only inspirational but is the reality of every successful person."

—Bishop Tudor Bismark, Sr. Pastor, New Life
Covenant Church, Zimbabwe; founder, Jabula
New Life Ministries International

"Pastor Elictia Hart brilliantly captures the essence of words much needed in the body of Christ today! The enemy uses many things, like fear, which come from a variety of giants or RED LIGHTS meant to keep us from fulfilling our purpose. But, by meditating on the words in *Redefining Red*, which echo God's truth from the Bible, you will discover that your greatest victories lie beyond your fears and red light moments. Indulge in this gem by Pastor Elictia and allow the Holy Spirit to change all your Red Lights into Green triumphant victories."

—Kevin and Chantell Davis, lead pastors,
River East London–South Africa

REDEFINING
RED

REDEFINING
RED

TURNING LIFE'S RED-LIGHT MOMENTS
INTO GREEN-LIGHT VICTORIES

ELICTIA HART

EMANATE
BOOKS

Published in Nashville, Tennessee, by Emanate Books, an imprint of Thomas Nelson. Emanate Books and Thomas Nelson are registered trademarks of HarperCollins Christian Publishing, Inc.

Thomas Nelson titles may be purchased in bulk for educational, business, fund-raising, or sales promotional use. For information, please e-mail SpecialMarkets@ThomasNelson.com.

Unless otherwise noted, Scripture quotations are taken from the Holy Bible, New International Version®, NIV®. Copyright © 1973, 1978, 1984, 2011 by Biblica, Inc.® Used by permission of Zondervan. All rights reserved worldwide. www.Zondervan.com. The "NIV" and "New International Version" are trademarks registered in the United States Patent and Trademark Office by Biblica, Inc.®

Scripture quotations marked ASV are from the Authorized Standard Version. Public domain.

Scripture quotations marked ESV are from the ESV® Bible (The Holy Bible, English Standard Version®). Copyright © 2001 by Crossway, a publishing ministry of Good News Publishers. Used by permission. All rights reserved.

Scripture quotations marked THE MESSAGE are from *The Message*. Copyright © by Eugene H. Peterson 1993, 1994, 1995, 1996, 2000, 2001, 2002. Used by permission of NavPress. All rights reserved. Represented by Tyndale House Publishers, Inc.

Scripture quotations marked NKJV are from the New King James Version®. © 1982 by Thomas Nelson. Used by permission. All rights reserved.

Scripture quotations marked NLT are from the Holy Bible, New Living Translation. © 1996, 2004, 2007, 2013, 2015 by Tyndale House Foundation. Used by permission of Tyndale House Publishers, Inc., Carol Stream, Illinois 60188. All rights reserved.

Scripture quotations marked TLB are from The Living Bible. Copyright © 1971. Used by permission of Tyndale House Publishers, Inc., Carol Stream, Illinois 60188. All rights reserved.

Any Internet addresses, phone numbers, or company or product information printed in this book are offered as a resource and are not intended in any way to be or to imply an endorsement by Thomas Nelson, nor does Thomas Nelson vouch for the existence, content, or services of these sites, phone numbers, companies, or products beyond the life of this book.

ISBN 978-0-7852-2365-8 (eBook)
ISBN 978-0-7852-2364-1 (TP)

Library of Congress Control Number: 2018943314

Printed in the United States of America

18 19 20 21 22   LSC   10 9 8 7 6 5 4 3 2 1

*I dedicate this book to my Lord and Savior,
Jesus. As I penned it I told Him, "Lord this is
YOUR book. Please use it to change lives."*

*To my greatest love, Jim, life with you is sweeter
every day. Thank you for loving me.
Micah and Jemma, you are my greatest joys!
Mom learns so much from you daily!*

*To you, the reader. May you see yourself throughout
the pages. May you embrace life's red-light moments,
understanding they can trigger green-light victories!
May your journey be one of* Redefining Red!

CONTENTS

CONTENTS

FOREWORD

When we talk about someone redefining a word, concept, or role, we usually mean they make it their own in a unique way that changes our understanding of it. My friend, sister in Christ, and partner in ministry Elictia Hart has done just that. In *Redefining Red*, Elictia takes a look at those red-light moments when we're tempted to stop in our tracks before running the other way and redefines them as green-means-go opportunities for us to grow in our faith and to strengthen our characters. And I can't think of anyone better qualified to redefine how we think of red than Elictia!

As a successful broadcast journalist, Elictia knows all about the pressure of those moments when the red light comes on. For her, it meant the camera was live and—ready or not—she was beamed into millions of viewers' screens around the world. Staying calm and in control in such moments isn't easy, and some people say you have to "fake it until you make it," meaning, just try to look like you've got it together whether you feel that way or not.

Elictia, on the other hand, teaches all of us to "faith it until we make it"—to trust God by stepping out in faith and not letting our feelings hold us back from the great things we're called to do. She reminds us that those moments when we feel weakest are the times when we learn to rely on God the most. Throughout the Bible we see this in how God's people faced red-light—or in Moses' case, *Red Sea*—situations.

Then as now, these times stretch our faith and force us to rely on God because we have no other option. As Elictia points out, though, we actually do have other options—ones that leave us mired in our fear, anxiety, stress, and inability to control life or resolve our problems. But as followers of Jesus Christ, we know the One who transforms all our mistakes, missteps, and might-have-beens into opportunities for redemption. So we do have a choice: we can fight or take flight—or we can step out in faith by trusting God.

Watching Elictia step away from her successful career as a broadcast journalist and to grow into her new roles as a wife, mother, and pastor, I know that she has definitely learned to trust God more. I know that Elictia practices what she preaches and brings the same passion she used to channel into her career to the forefront of her love for God, for her family, and for her ministry.

Her example and the many examples she points out in Scripture inspire us all. No matter what you may be facing or where you are in life, you *will* have red-light moments. But as Elictia shows us in this wonderful book, we have a choice about how we respond. As tempting as it may be to panic, to run, or to fight, she forces us to realize that these moments may be the doorways to growth we've been looking for. If we're willing to walk by faith and to trust God each step of the way, then we, like Elictia, can experience the joy of *Redefining Red*!

Samuel Rodriguez
President, National Hispanic Christian
Leadership Conference (NHCLC)
Lead Pastor, New Season

CHAPTER 1

RED IS THE NEW GREEN

REDEFINING RED WHEN YOU'RE DREAMING

*Each of us has an inner dream that
we can unfold if we will just have
the courage to admit what it is.*

—Julia Cameron

What in the world was I doing? Why did I ever think I could do this? And a better question: *How* would I get through this? What if I froze in front of the camera and couldn't say anything?

"Get ready, Elictia! You're on in . . . five!"

I nodded and adjusted the cordless mic in my sweaty palm.

1

Had I worn the right outfit? Should I have worn the blue blouse instead? Did I look as terrified as I felt? Was my makeup still okay?

"Four!"

My heart pounded against my chest like a jackhammer. I tried to swallow but my mouth was too dry, sending another wave of nausea-inducing panic through me. *Please, Lord*, I silently prayed, *help me through this! I can't do this—but I know You can.*

"Three!"

Adjusting my stance and the angle of my head, I forced myself to smile—not too big, but a pleasant, professional expression of confidence. I cleared my throat one more time, grateful that my voice might work after all.

"Two!"

Oh, dear God, be with me! I was about to go live before several hundred thousand—maybe more than a million—viewers for the first time. All those college classes, countless rehearsals, and dozens of videotaped segments no longer mattered. Looking into that big eye of the camera, I was about to be seen in houses, apartments, gas stations, schools, hospitals, and offices all around the Tri-Cities area of the Pacific Northwest. I was going inside the daily lives of viewers everywhere to tell them about— *what was my segment about?*

Silence. Only my cameraman's one finger folding in on itself as the red light of his shouldered camera began glowing brighter than Rudolph's nose. *Breathe, girl, breathe!*

"Thanks, Bob," I said right into the camera. "As you can see, I'm here in Yakima outside the airport's newly completed expansion . . ."

From there, I'm not sure what I said, but I know I kept talking. Back then reporters doing live stories didn't have smartphones, tablets, or other note-taking gadgets. We occasionally wrote down names or direct quotes, but the story was mostly all in my head. As my sixty seconds ticked away, my cameraman signaled me it was time to transition to the pre-taped, pre-edited piece we'd shot that morning.

"So let's take a look inside the newly renovated terminal."

While the taped piece of me walking from one gate to another inside the Yakima airport ran, I tried to relax and catch my breath, knowing that in exactly sixty seconds, I would be back on air to close the segment. All I had to do was say the final two sentences I'd written and memorized, say my name, and close and toss back to our studio anchor. And I must have done it, but I honestly can't remember anything but the red glow perched atop the camera.

I had just learned, contrary to everything I'd been taught since childhood, that I would have to redefine my perception of red.

FINDING MY SCRIPT

Looking back, almost thirty years later, I still recall how unbelievably nervous I felt then and how the Lord got me through it. I know my first on-air report was far from perfect, but I had to start somewhere. Everyone in the industry had told me that the best confidence builder is experience. Which sounded good until I realized that was my problem—I didn't have any! In fact, at the time I wasn't sure I even wanted to be a broadcast journalist.

You know how some people always knew they wanted to be a doctor or nurse, a teacher or lawyer, an artist or performer? Well, I wasn't one of those. I had no idea what I wanted to do. Growing up as a Pacific Northwest girl, I stayed close to home and attended the University of Washington. (Go Huskies!) For the first few years of college I just learned to go with the flow. I didn't have a clear picture of what my adult life would look like, so I just studied and kept asking the Lord, "What classes should I take? What career field should I explore?"

Going into my third year in college, I finally had to declare my major. At this time, when I was still not 100 percent certain, I believe God gently guided and nudged me in the right direction by allowing me to get a job at the *Seattle Times*. I thought, *Oh, this will be great! Media is exciting, and I love to write, so this should be fun.*

Only it wasn't.

After working there for a time, I realized that I *didn't* want to do print journalism. It just wasn't me. The constant pressure to have everything written, edited, polished, and ready to go never stopped. And the very best journalists for the paper became victims of their own success, constantly forced to write more and longer articles. The energy, the vibe, the whole role was just not a fit for me.

Coming off that disappointment, I was a little wary to try another media job, but I couldn't say no when offered an internship with KOMO-TV, the ABC affiliate in Seattle. As soon as I stepped into the newsroom, I felt at home. People were scrambling, phones were ringing, keyboards were clicking, and editors were shouting out last-minute instructions to reporters and the camera crew as they rushed out the door to cover breaking stories.

Just then the lady guiding me on a tour of the newsroom asked me to wait while she handled a breaking-news situation requiring her immediate attention. I just stood there taking it all in, watching everything in slow motion, as I thought, *This is it!*

This is what I want to do! But even as that thought popped into mind, I wondered if I had what it took to be a broadcast journalist, or "talent" as the reporters and anchors were dubbed by the rest of the studio team.

The following week I began my journey to find out. Grateful for such a cool internship at a TV station, I was not above doing any job and soon found myself working frantically behind the scenes. I began answering phones, taking notes at meetings, preparing the sheets (scripts) that the main anchors would refer to if the prompter went down, and doing any grunt work below the veteran workers' pay grades. I totally owned it and loved every minute of it! (Today most stations use iPads or some type of electronic device for their scripts.)

But I knew I had to take the risk to find out.

RED MEANS GO

As my internship became a full-time job, my dream of becoming a broadcast journalist came to life. I believe the seed of that dream was already inside me, and the nourishment of working in that environment caused it to grow. The more I learned, the more I knew this was what God had created me to do for this season of my life. I still got nervous, especially as I worked through all those firsts—my first time on-air, my first time reporting live, my first time improvising at an event, but I realized that growth only came with experience. And experience only came with being nervous and making mistakes.

During this time of growth, as my dream matured, I was amazed at how God often used other people to encourage and empower my dream. After working as a "reporter at large" for the station where I had interned, I began working my way up the ranks in a variety of roles, each one providing unique experience in the world of broadcast journalism. I worked as a field producer, news scriptwriter, fact checker, video editor, and compiler of financial data from the stock market. Finally, I began to get on-air experience at a station in Kansas, invaluable practice to help me work the kinks out and become more comfortable in front of the blinking red eye of the camera. After a couple of years bouncing around like this, I put together a tape of my best clips and was hired as a weekend sports anchor at a television station in Mississippi.

Mitch, the sports director there, was one of the most influential bosses I have ever had the pleasure of knowing and working for. When I interviewed, I didn't know that God was sending me a boss who was a man of God, but Mitch constantly preached the Word to me, sometimes literally, other times through his words and actions.

Mitch continually deposited encouragement that helped shape me as a reporter and allowed me to reach and dream for the future. I recall being on a 5:00 p.m. live shot outside and being a little unnerved because it was storming badly. I not only had that little red light winking at me, I had wind and rain slamming against me. While I wasn't in any danger, I was distracted, annoyed, and frustrated. I made it through the first time, but I felt shaky and began doubting myself.

Seeing my less-than-stellar performance the first time, Mitch phoned before the next live shot at 6:00 p.m. and told my photographer to patch him through to me. Suddenly, I couldn't see him but I could hear him. "Elictia," he said, in his thick, Southern accent. "Listen to me: you are in *your* season, at the right place, at the right time. God has placed you there. Now you do that live shot like nobody's business. Do not be moved by the weather!"

With that encouragement, when it came time for the 6:00 p.m. live shot, I "sang and danced" in the storm and did an excellent job. With Mitch's encouragement and reminder that God was in control, I could now see myself doing live shots unaffected by my surroundings. I could visualize myself doing larger assignments after this moment of learning. I understood the way I was allowing circumstances—in this case, the bad weather—to influence my attitude. But when I visualized myself moving forward toward my dream by persevering through adversity, it was a game changer.

Seeing red doesn't mean you should stop.

It only means you need to let the Lord lead you forward.

Which brings me back to you. I know with certainty that if your eyes are reading these pages, it's not by chance. This book has landed in your hands purposefully. I'm humbled and privileged to share some of my journey with you in hopes that you can glean from what I've experienced and how God has worked in my life.

I've learned that you don't have to be in front of a television camera to encounter those "redefining red" moments. Everyone has them, and our lives often have more of them than we would like. Times when red feels like bloodshed as you're facing your fears. Situations when a red spark of possibility signifies your desperation for the provision of fire. Places where you feel lost, glimpsing red reflectors along a deserted roadside. Moments that haunt you with the scarlet letter of shame as past events try to derail your destiny.

You see, redefining red only means that it's time to be "on" when the camera goes live. This same strategy applies when you're faced with your life's most tumultuous trials and most devastating disasters. When you face one of life's red moments, you may be tempted to freeze in place, paralyzed by fear, doubt, uncertainty, and anxiety. When you're faced with a red moment, however, it's not the time to step back, stay down, or sit out. When a red light goes off in your life, signaling something unexpected, challenging, and frightening, you must step out in faith and go to God. Life's red lights should be a green light for us to run to the arms of our Father!

He will give you His power to shine through your weaknesses and His strength to sustain you when you can't go on. The apostle Paul knew about this kind of divine reinforcement firsthand. Paul apparently struggled with some problem or issue that he deemed a "thorn in my flesh" (2 Cor. 12:7), his own personal red light. He prayed fervently and repeatedly for the Lord to remove this thorn before God finally told him, "My grace is sufficient for you, for my power is made perfect in weakness" (v. 9).

RED ALERT

Throughout this book we will explore a variety of redefining-red moments, from both my life and the examples of heroes from the Bible. With each one, we will discover our red moments can become green lights for trusting God and embracing our divine destiny. Red truly is the new green! If we rely on our own power, we may be tempted to panic, give up, or lose hope. But when we run to God and rely on Him, we're empowered for the greatness for which He created us as His children.

God is faithful to meet us wherever we find ourselves. His

grace, mercy, strength, and power are available to us in the midst of places we never expected to be—when we face an illness or injury, lose our jobs, experience a betrayal, or wrestle with the consequences of past mistakes. These red moments cannot rob us of the riches of our Father's heavenly glory. When you feel pushed to the limit and up against a wall, that's when you can trust God not only catch to you but hold you close.

So many people have no idea what they're capable of accomplishing and what God has created them to achieve with Him as their power source. Unfortunately, they often wait until they're faced with an excruciating loss or painful setback to draw on the resources they need in order to overcome, both within themselves and from their Creator. But these red-flag occasions can often become red-letter opportunities, strengthening our spiritual muscles and equipping us for greater goals ahead.

I know firsthand that if God can use me, He can use you. To achieve His greatness and advance His kingdom, you only have to be willing. One thing I quickly learned about being on-air talent—you often have to improvise! With breaking news, there's often not enough time to do research, develop main points, or frame a story. I had to be willing to think on the fly, do the best I could, and keep going.

Similarly, our lives often require this kind of improvisation, stepping out in faith when we can't see what's ahead or how we'll get there. But as we learn from various examples in the Bible, God delights in using underdogs. You don't have to have your act together, have enough experience, or lead a perfect life for Him to use you, strengthen you, and delight in you. God has planted a dream inside you and wants to help you grow with it. And the amazing thing about this growth process is the way He often turns adversity into fertilizer, feeding your dream until it's time for you to bloom.

A DREAM COME TRUE

While the Bible tells us about many dreamers, one in particular always reminds me of the way God uses our struggles to make us stronger. Consider Joseph, son of Jacob, grandson of Isaac and great-grandson of Abraham. You can read all about the one the Bible refers to as "the dreamer" in Genesis, chapters 37 to 50.

Joseph was just seventeen years old when God gave him dreams—two dreams to be exact. In these dreams God showed Joseph he would be honored by his family as a powerful leader and that even people of other nations would bow to him. The thing was, Joseph's brothers were already jealous of him for being the youngest and their father's favorite. When Joseph shared his dreams with them, they wanted to kill him. And they almost did. But they opted to sell him into slavery instead.

Talk about getting off to a rocky start!

Ever felt like you were worlds away from realizing your dreams? Like there was no way, no possibility that your dream could be realized in the midst of all you're experiencing? Rest assured, even those of us who have seen our dreams come to pass have often felt this way. It's so tempting when our dreams don't happen quickly and easily to assume, "Oh well, this dream was only that—a dream. It's never going to come to pass, so I might as well give up and move on."

Surely Joseph must have wondered if his dreams were going to be realized as he ricocheted from one terrible circumstance to another. For thirteen years this young man struggled through the consequences of his brothers' betrayal. And as if that wasn't bad enough, Joseph was then framed by his boss's wife and sent to prison. We're probably safe in suspecting that somewhere in all of this Joseph must have felt he missed it . . . that these were not dreams that would ever come to pass, just flights of fancy crash-landing with his new life as a convict in Egypt. His circumstances were so completely opposite of what he dreamed.

How about you? Do you feel like you're moving in the direction of your dreams, growing closer to realizing all that God has planted in your heart? Do you feel like your dreams are in located in Miami and you're hitchhiking from Seattle? In other words, are you so far from seeing them realized that you're at a place of feeling like you completely missed it? But what if you were still going to reach your destination, just not by the most direct route, not the path you would map for yourself?

Joseph didn't see his dreams come to pass until he was thirty years old. That's when Joseph's ability to interpret dreams got noticed by Pharaoh, whose sleep had been troubled. Joseph explained the way Pharaoh's dream revealed what the future would hold: seven years of bountiful harvests followed by seven years of famine. The ruler of Egypt was so impressed with this Jewish felon that he made Joseph second in command, responsible for preparing for the famine to come.

And when the famine came, guess who crawled down to Egypt looking for food? Joseph's brothers! They didn't recognize him at first, and Joseph had a little fun with them before revealing the truth. But Joseph forgave them because he could finally see how God had transformed all the terrible events in his life into trophies of God's grace. As Joseph explained to his family, "You intended to harm me, but God intended it for good to accomplish what is now being done, the saving of many lives" (Gen. 50:20).

. LISTEN UP

Joseph reminds us all that God keeps His promises to us. If God gave you a dream, like Joseph, He will see to it that it happens. No one can hinder it from happening except—and this is a big "except"—us: you and me. That's right; we are the ones who can keep our God-given dreams from being realized. So we must be diligent about doing our best to walk out this life like God's Word asks. Then we can count on God to do what He has promised. In the Bible, He tells us His Word will never return void, but it will accomplish that which He has sent for it to do (Isa. 55:11, paraphrased). Wow. He's saying, "If I said it, then so it shall be!" How exciting is that!

Just like He gave Joseph dreams, God is still in the business of giving us dreams. He may deliver these in a number of different ways. God may actually give you dreams when you sleep, just as He gave Joseph. Over the years God has given me dreams that I have had the pleasure of watching come to fruition. It's completely amazing to have a dream and then be able to watch it unfold right in front of you.

Sometimes God gives us visions. In these situations, the best way I know to describe the experience is that you're awake but daydreaming. He might also reveal a dream by showing someone something about you and they share it with you. The Bible tells us God is always speaking, wanting to reveal things to us (Heb. 1:1–2; John 10:27; 2 Tim. 3:16; James 3:17). But are we listening?

You see, whatever method our heavenly Father uses, He will likely confirm it through another source. You may be sitting in the break room at work and someone may come up out of the blue and begin talking about the very thing God has revealed to you. You may be at the gym, at a church service, or listening to the radio. God is so powerful and all-knowing, He can use anyone and anything to speak to us. Are you diligently listening—and then are you acting on what you hear?

From my experience, this process of hearing and acting is often how my dreams grew to fruition. I learned a lot about myself during those early days of my career. It's so important to learn who you are, what makes you tick, and what you are passionate about—essentially what you get excited about doing. Typically whatever you are passionate about won't feel like work. And if you are passionate about something, you will want to do it; you will work hard at it and not get drained because it's part of your DNA. God has made you passionate about it.

Even though I discovered broadcast journalism late in my college career, I had always enjoyed talking with people and discussing significant topics. I enjoyed doing research and writing out my ideas and opinions. I liked performing and being part of a team. All these talents and abilities combined to be fully utilized in my role as a reporter, anchor, and TV personality. The more I trusted God with bringing my dream to life, the more I could enjoy the process of being who He made me to be.

The same is true for you. Your heavenly Father knows what He's doing. When God created you, He gave you unique talents and a specific personal purpose. Alongside those talents and purpose He gave you passion. When you connect the dots from talents to passion, you begin to see the design of your divine purpose.

PRACTICE MAKES PERFECT

Identifying your talents and what you're passionate about doesn't mean you won't have to hone your abilities or practice to get better. Quite the contrary; when you work on something you are a little bit good at, you will get better at it. The more you put into it, the better you will be. We have all heard the saying, "Practice makes perfect," which is not entirely true, but good advice nonetheless. While we may never be completely perfect in this life, we will definitely be better and better, and in some cases we can master certain elements of our skills.

Here's the thing, though: most of the time, when you are skilled and talented in an area that you were created to work in, you will have a desire to do it, and often that desire can become your passion. Think about it. Most people who are at the top of what they do, whether they are athletes or airplane pilots or doctors, were good at what they did a long time before they reached the top. They had skills in a particular sport, in aviation, or in science. These skills created interest to further delve into their particular field, and soon they had a passion to be the best in their field.

You may be saying, "Well, when I was younger I was good at certain things. But it's too late now." Hold on a minute, my friend! If you were good at it then, chances are you arc probably still good at it. Now I'm not saying you can be an Olympic gymnast at forty-five. For some things there are seasons. Even most athletes have seasons when they can crank out the best of their particular sport. But you can still coach gymnastics or do something associated with that field if that's your passion. You just have to be creative and ask God to guide you. Trust me, He *loves* to give guidance.

Take a second right now and think of the top three things

you are really good at doing. Things you know are your strengths and talents. Jot your talents down in the margin. You should be extremely passionate about these things you're good at. Or you may feel a little embarrassed and unsure, unwilling to brag or have others know your secret talents. Either way, though, God created you to do these things well. And as you embrace what you're good at doing, what you're passionate about pursuing, then you can trust that God will provide everything you need each step of the way.

But it all starts with keeping your dream alive and trusting God to help it grow. You have to see yourself where you are going. And right smack dab in the middle of your seeing yourself there, God will often promote you to that place. But here's the problem: if you can't see yourself there, it can be that much harder to actually arrive at your destination. So don't shut off those visions, your dreams, and that small voice saying, "This is where you are going."

I, too, had to first see myself in whatever television job I wanted to get. I had to see myself as a producer, reporter, then an anchor in order to actually achieve these positions. I had to stretch my imagination to think long-term and envision myself on a network program somewhere. I didn't know at the time which network—I just had to visualize myself growing, advancing, bringing the dream to life. If I didn't see myself there, how could I actually arrive at that destination?

So think about it. Can you actually see yourself down the road in that place that seems unachievable, in that place that seems miles away? Or do you feel blindsided by obstacles that continually seem to block your path? Does red mean go for you, or has red stopped you in your tracks?

No matter where you are in life right now, no matter where you are in your relationship with God, ask Him to rekindle the flame of your dreams. Trust Him to transform your struggles, mistakes, and disappointments into spiritual muscle to reach even higher and run even faster. Believe that God's strength is made perfect in your weakness.

Start redefining red! Red doesn't have to be a stop sign—it's your green light to go to God!

SHIFTING RED MOMENTS TO GREEN TRIUMPHS

GO DEEPER

Where are you on the journey toward your current dream? What is the next step you need to take in order to move closer to where God is calling you? Before you can realize your dream, you have to figure out what the next step is in that direction. Process is critical on this journey toward your destiny and purpose. Ask God to show you where you are and where to go with your next steps.

GO FURTHER

In a journal or a notebook, write the three things you know you are great at. Then write down what makes you good and why you think you are good at these things. How much time are you currently spending each day (or even each week) exercising these three abilities? Which one do you feel most drawn to pursue in your current season of life?

CHAPTER 2

FACING THE FIRE

REDEFINING RED WHEN
YOU'RE AFRAID

Fear of failure must never be a
reason not to try something.

—Frederick Smith

My family and I were traveling on a road trip a while ago and began playing I Spy to pass the time. It was my husband's turn, and he said, "I spy something . . . red." Our twins, Jemma and Micah, were about seven at the time and immediately started looking all around as our car slowed for traffic. Then Jemma blurted, "I know what it is!"

"What?" I asked, curious to know myself.

"There it is—right there! You know, that thing dogs pee on!"

We swiftly turned to where Jemma was pointing—at a fire

hydrant—and began laughing until we cried. She had no idea what to call it, but she recognized it by the context where she was used to seeing it, as a canine porta potty!

After our laughter subsided, I reflected on the incredible lesson beneath her innocent observation: how you perceive something will determine how you interpret it. My daughter interpreted the fire hydrant as a place where dogs relieve themselves, which obviously isn't worth very much. Well, except for a good laugh in our case.

As I continued to think, however, I realized our perceptions also shape the value we place on what we're seeing. Fire hydrants are precious facilities—invaluable when a fire occurs. But since Jemma couldn't identify a hydrant by its true purpose, she mistakenly assumed it only related to our pet lifting a leg. The hydrant would have no value to her if a fire broke out, because she couldn't see it for what it really is—and the incredible potential it has for saving lives.

From there, my thoughts drifted to fires, and I realized that the context and our past experiences often influence how we see them as well. If you turn a corner and see a blazing campfire, you're likely to look for marshmallows to make s'mores. But if you come around the corner and see flames consuming the second story of your house, then you'll be calling 911 for a fire truck and hoping there's one of Jemma's hydrants nearby.

Fire has the power to provide warmth, cook our food, and illuminate a dark night. Of course, it also has the power to destroy homes and buildings, ravage forests, and claim human lives. It all depends on how it's contained and utilized—which brings me back to our perceptions.

I suspect we often see most opportunities in our lives the

same way my daughter viewed that hydrant. Our perceptions are colored by what we know—or more likely, don't know—about the situation. When there's conflict, uncertainty, and fear, we tend to let the stress of the situation overwhelm us and possibly prevent us from moving forward. Only when we're grounded in God's truth and relying on Him to guide us can we face the fires in our lives. Only when we place our faith in Him can we discover that red means go when we're afraid.

GETTING INTO THE GAME

I learned this lesson repeatedly during the early years of my broadcasting career. In fact, I will never forget a pressure-filled situation that propelled me into my destiny during that season of my life. After working as a writer, feature producer, and then feature reporter for FOX Sports, I longed to advance to the next level and cover major events for FOX Sports. I remember explaining to a friend, "I don't want to tell everybody what happened at the game later. I want to work at the actual game. I want to cover the game. I need to be there. I want to get off the sidelines and into the game!"

As I began exploring what I needed to do to make this happen, I went to my boss and asked him who I needed to call to get in at FOX Sports. He hesitated at first but then gave me the name of one of the most respected men in the business, Roy Hamilton. Mr. Hamilton was in upper management at Fox Sports and had been in the business for nearly twenty years. His eye for excellence in broadcasting, raising up and bringing out the best in talent, along with his no-nonsense approach gained him the utmost respect within the television sports world. My boss cautioned me that Mr. Hamilton was quite busy so to be prepared to make good use of the time I would be able to get with him, if any.

"That's fine," I said, trying to put on a brave face. "I can handle it."

But as I mentioned the name to some of my other colleagues, I would ask, "Have you ever heard of a gentleman in our industry named Roy Hamilton? I'm scheduling a call and wonder what he's like."

Repeatedly I heard: "Ooh, you're supposed to be calling him? He's one of the big guns. If you get in to see him, have your stuff together. He means business and rightfully so, he knows what he is doing."

I soon discovered everybody knew Mr. Roy Hamilton. He was a vice president at FOX Sports and known for being extremely brilliant, bringing out the best in others and doing things his way with the ultimate outcome always impressing viewers. The more I learned about Mr. Hamilton, the more I wondered if I would be good enough to work for him. Maybe I should just wait a few more months, or maybe even until next year when I had a bit more experience under my belt.

Why rock the boat, right? Was I really prepared to work at the next level? Would he tell me I was too inexperienced to cover live games? But then again, I knew nothing would happen if I didn't at least make the call. The Lord had stirred something in my heart for a reason, and now I had a next step—the least I could do was take it. Even if that meant tripping.

When I put in that phone call to Mr. Hamilton, boy, was I nervous. I felt like Dorothy calling to make an appointment with the Wizard of Oz—or maybe even the Wicked Witch! I knew enough of how corporate life worked to expect that I would only get through to his personal assistant initially. He was far too busy and important to take a cold call from some newbie reporter he'd never heard of before. Still, I told myself, *That's okay. I'll connect with someone from his team, and he'll get my message and call me back. Why? Because I have favor with God. And if Mr. Hamilton never calls me back? Well, I still have favor with God!* I worked hard to make it a win-win instead of the lost cause projected by my fears.

As expected, I got his secretary and left that all-too-common message while my stomach was turning somersaults inside me. Then I waited. And waited. And probably waited some more. It was actually less than twenty-four hours because he called me back the very next day!

I was in the tape vault pulling up old video on Hank Aaron to do a story for Keith Olbermann when my pager went off. (Yep, we were still in the pager days!) Realizing it was one of the FOX numbers, I thought, *Oh, my goodness, what am I gonna say? It's Roy Hamilton! Stay cool, Elictia. Stay cool. And don't forget to breathe.* So I turned to my colleagues and said, "I'll be back, you guys." And then added, "Pray for me. Pray for me!" as I headed out the door to call him back.

"Hello. May I speak to Roy Hamilton, please?" I said, ducking into an empty conference room. I was transferred after his assistant confirmed who I was and what I wanted.

"Roy Hamilton," I heard over the line. His confident, deep voice caused me to suddenly shake in my boots, or high heels, as it was. Knowing that usually you only have one chance to make a good impression, I prayed, *Come on, God, You're gonna have to do what You want to do right now in this place, in this moment, because I'm about to fail this mini-interview conversation.*

"Yes, this is Elictia . . ." Oh, no! My voice sounded small.

"Yes, I got your initial call. What can I do for you, Elictia?" He was direct and to the point, no small talk. Why wouldn't he be, he was ultra-important and had plenty of other things he could be doing I'm certain. I mean, honestly I was grateful he even called me back. I bet a lot of executives in his position would not have given me the time of day. So to be frank, I was extremely lucky to have him on the other end of my phone. I could feel every bit of his authoritative power coursing through that phone line.

"Yes, right, thank you. I was told that you're the person responsible for assigning talent to game coverage . . . uh, is that correct?" I was stuttering and stammering all over the place, already failing miserably.

"Correct," he said.

He went on to explain a bit about what he did. Which was so much! Wow, and he was chatting with little me! He checked his calendar and asked if I could come over to his office the next day at noon. He told me to bring everything I knew to bring, including all the knowledge I had accumulated over time. We wrapped up the conversation by saying goodbye. I was frozen as I hung up the phone thinking I didn't say any of the right things. I felt like I had gotten fired before I was even hired. I'm not sure why I felt this way. I think I was just overwhelmed with it all. I had just spoken to "the" Roy Hamilton!

Walking back into the video vault, I felt like I had just missed a golden opportunity, like I had a winning ticket and watched it slip out of my fingers. But as I replayed the conversation in my head, I realized that the real test was still to come. Meeting him in person would be what determined whether I reached my goal. I had to find some way to channel all the pressure I felt in a positive direction. I could still rise to the occasion and refuse to let my fear change the course of what the Lord might have for me. I knew that if God opened the door, no one could close it— except me!

PRESSURE REQUIRES PERSEVERANCE

The next day I went to Mr. Hamilton's office. I remember walking in, sweaty palms and all, while trying to look the part of a talented, confident broadcast journalist that he would definitely want to hire. His assistant showed me into his office, and he stood to shake my hand before offering me a seat across from his desk.

"I brought this tape for you with some of my strongest work," I said. "And here's a hard copy of my résumé, along with several articles and scripts I've written."

"Great," he said, taking the tape and file folder and tossing it on a credenza behind his desk. He asked me a few questions about myself. He seemed genuinely interested in my career. Then he gave me some instructions: "Here's what I want you to do. I want you to make a tease about NFL Europe. You have three days to do it, and then bring it back to me."

He added, "You have to make it good."

In a very sincere way he told me I had one chance to pass or fail. We both chuckled. Mine, of course, was a nervous, oh my goodness, chuckle. Then he told me it was nice to meet me and he looked forward to seeing my work. I gathered my items and left, already thinking about what work was in front of me.

The whole meeting couldn't have lasted more than twenty-five minutes. It is hilarious to recall how nervous I was over a meeting that was nothing but a blurred conversation and handshake. I was so grateful for his time but I was now extremely nervous. At the end of the day, I didn't know if I was good enough to do what he was asking of me. Mr. Hamilton had a sure-fire test he relied on, and I was about to take it. And I knew it wouldn't be easy.

I knew nothing about NFL Europe—no one did! Adding to my impossible task was the fact that it was a tease, a ten- to twenty-second quick cut that teases a big story coming up. You know, those segments when you're watching a show or ballgame and the local anchor pops in and says, "Coming up—two people were shot at Bridgeport Mall and remain in critical condition. Details at eleven!" These teases try to pique interest in a big story so viewers will tune in to get the full report.

I felt pressured from every angle: I had a challenging topic that the viewers and I knew nothing about, brief on-air time, and a very short turnaround time to produce a unique, professional-quality clip. Mr. Hamilton's words haunted me. I had one chance to pass or fail. And it all came down to a ten-to-twenty-second tease—at least it felt like it did at that time.

The first day I became overwhelmed with research and the history of the fledgling NFL Europe organization. There was no way this would be my best work, and yet the future of my entire career seemed to rest on it. The next morning, I knew I would stress myself into a state of fearful paralysis if I kept focusing on the pressure. So instead I took a deep breath and said to myself,

"Okay, here we go. All glory to God. I can do this. Inspire me, Lord. Show me the way. You've got this."

Three days later I returned to Mr. Hamilton's office and handed him my tape. He thanked me and said, "Okay, so how do you think you did?"

"It's great," I said, as confidently as possible. "I'm really proud of it. I put everything I have into it."

"Am I going to like it?" he asked with his eyes locked to mine. He was trying to see whether I really believed in myself and my work or if I was just blowing smoke.

"You're going to love it. It's an awesome tease."

"Am I going to put it on the air?" he continued.

"Yes, you will," I said without hesitation.

"Okay, let's have a look."

He inserted the tape and turned to watch the screen above it. I tried to look like I was watching it with him but I really just wanted to watch him. He did not move; I don't know if he even breathed. Nor did I. When it was over, he said, "Do you really think it was good?"

"Well, I mean, it was solid . . . but it could've been better."

"It can always be better, you're right," he said. And he began to explain all the things I could have done differently from A to Z. He told me all the problems with my approach. Why it wasn't good and wouldn't be put on air. What it needed to be memorable and worthy of being aired. All the things that he could probably do in his sleep because he was so good at this type of thing.

My heart stopped while everything else in my body quivered. But I sat there and took in all his wisdom, and I accepted his critique. I knew to advance in my career, I would have to up my game. While his analysis felt harsh, it wasn't mean-spirited at all, in fact, quite the opposite. He genuinely cared and I believe that's why he took the time to explain it all. Everything he said, I hadn't considered.

"I'll give you another chance," he said. "Two days—a do-over. Bring it back. You can do this but you have to dig in and try harder."

In that moment, I was crushed. I honestly didn't know how I could make that tease any better.

But I did.

After making an entirely new clip, I got the job! And you know why I got that job? Much later, Roy told me, "Because of the way you responded, I knew you were teachable. You were willing to risk facing the fire to hear what I had to say, without running away. Your skills were excellent, and your initial tease was very, very good. In fact, we aired it! But here's the thing, your skills would only take you so far. There are plenty of good reporters who can do the job, but not all of them are willing to overcome their fears and become teachable." He had actually been messing with me when he "disliked" my original clip—as he said, he broadcasted it! He simply wanted to see how I would handle criticism; he wanted to know if I was teachable, humble, and flexible.

This was part of Mr. Hamilton's brilliance. He could cultivate, recognize, and enhance someone's potential. It was because of him that I ended up going on air as an anchor. He saw my potential and pushed me to do more. This was one vice president who was much more than a boss, he would forever impact my life and it all began with my learning that being teachable was the door that stood between success and failure. Mr. Roy Hamilton helped me redefine red in that season!

LIGHT MY FIRE

That story still causes my stomach to clench, but it also brings a smile to my face. I would never have improved my abilities and realized my full potential as a network sports reporter and anchor without going through the fire and being tested by Mr. Roy Hamilton. From that experience, I learned that not only did I have to believe in myself, but I also had to trust God with the outcome. I had to follow the Lord's guidance, do my best, and then step out in faith, trusting one way or another everything would be okay.

I'm certainly not the only one who has grown through such a stressful situation. You probably have your own experiences that have forced you to confront your fears and deepen your faith in God. And we certainly see plenty of these moments in the Bible. In fact, perhaps one of the best stories of handling pressure by trusting God involves facing the fire—literally. You might be familiar with the story of Meshach, Shadrach, and Abednego, three Jewish young men forced to endure a burning furnace because they refused to give in to their Babylonian captors.

Along with the entire Jewish nation, including their friend Daniel, these three men were held as prisoners in Babylon, a violent and pagan nation that had conquered the tribes of Judah and Israel. (We find their story in the book of Daniel in the Old Testament.) The people ended up being held captive for seventy years, and during this time they were frequently tested by their conquerors, initially led by King Nebuchadnezzar. While he admired their devout faith and national pride, the king wanted to assimilate them into his own culture. And one of his boldest attempts involved getting them to change who, and how, they worshipped.

Wow. Can you imagine facing a test with such dire consequences? This was truly a matter of life and death. Daniel was exempt only because he had already impressed the king so much that Nebuchadnezzar appointed Daniel to a position in the king's royal court. But Daniel's three friends were required to attend the official dedication of this gold-plated, ninety-foot statue of the king. While it was basically just a huge wooden pole coated with gold, from a distance it must have looked like the Space Needle!

After the Babylonian officials gathered, they were told that when the music started, they had to bow down and worship this golden image of the king. If they didn't, they would be thrown into a fiery furnace. Daniel's three friends faced an ugly ultimatum: renounce their religion and their God and pledge their allegiance to their captors' god.

For them, it was an easy choice. They said, "King Nebuchadnezzar, we do not need to defend ourselves before you in this matter. If we are thrown into the blazing furnace, the God we serve is able to deliver us from it, and he will deliver us from Your Majesty's hand. But even if he does not, we want you to know, Your Majesty, that we will not serve your gods or worship the image of gold you have set up" (Dan. 3:16–18).

Talk about staying cool while facing the fire! Notice they didn't lead a rebellion, plan a boycott, condemn the king for building his idol, or argue about why they shouldn't have to bow down. In fact, they actually told Nebuchadnezzar they didn't need to defend their decision. They essentially said, "First off, our God *is* able, but if He doesn't deliver us, we will not bow. Even if it means we burn to death." I love their faith! I call that "but-if-not faith." They trusted the Lord to rescue them—and pointed out that even if He didn't, they still would not regret their decision. They trusted God beyond just their present circumstances. As much as they wanted to live and trusted God would protect them, they knew it would be okay even if they didn't emerge alive out of the king's furnace.

They were arrested and taken before Nebuchadnezzar who was "furious with rage" (v. 13). He told them he would give them one more chance to bow down. If they did not, they would be burned alive because "what god will be able to rescue you from my hand?" (v. 15). When they refused, the king ordered the furnace heated *seven times* hotter than usual, commanded his strongest soldiers to tie them up fully clothed, and then had the three young men dropped into the deadly incinerator. In fact, the flames actually killed the men who threw Meshach, Shadrach, and Abednego into the furnace.

But they didn't even break a sweat! Expecting to see the young men burned to ashes, Nebuchadnezzar instead asked his guards, "Weren't there three men that we tied up and threw into the fire? . . . Look! I see four men walking around in the fire, unbound and unharmed, and the fourth looks like a son of the gods" (vv. 24–25). God Himself had shown up! He walked in the midst of the fire with His faithful children. This is a lesson for you and me to remember.

We can wrap our confidence around God's promises, and when He allows us to experience a fiery furnace, God promises to be there with us (Ps. 23:4; Isa. 43:1–2). Why? Because He loves us! Even the king was forced to recognize the power of the one true, living God: "Praise be to the God of Shadrach, Meshach and Abednego, who has sent his angel and rescued his servants!" (v. 28). God was glorified, and His servants were recognized for their total faith in Him.

PRESSURIZE YOUR FAITH

My fears of failing the test for my promotion cannot compare to the life-or-death test that Shadrach, Meshach, and Abednego faced. But their miraculous story reminds us that even in the most extreme circumstances, we must never allow our fear to eclipse our faith. In fact, I'm convinced pressure, stress, and fear can sometimes help us accomplish our God-given dreams. How? Because they force us to depend on Him.

I love how the Bible explains this process of strengthening our faith by pressurizing it:

> You know that under pressure, your faith-life is forced into the open and shows its true colors. So don't try to get out of anything prematurely. Let it do its work so you become mature and well-developed, not deficient in any way. If you don't know what you're doing, pray to the Father. He loves to help. You'll get his help, and won't be condescended to when you ask for it. (James 1:3–5 THE MESSAGE)

After doing a little research, I discovered the Greek word used in Scripture that we translate as "pressure" here literally means to use force, might, strength, and violence. Think about the way the air pressure changes when we fly and reach a higher altitude. Or consider the pressure of the ocean depths that swimmers must adjust to when they go deep-sea diving. These examples show how pressure directly influences our senses. We can't hear so well up at thirty thousand feet or when we're a quarter mile underwater. Even our vision can be impaired, along with our breathing, of course.

Pressure, emotional and psychological, can also affect our judgment. If we are faced with lots of pressures or stressors, it's going to affect our judgment and how we go about responding to a situation. For instance, if someone were to come up to you with a gun, there's going to be a certain amount of circumstantial pressure on you. And as a result, your thought process and judgment may not be as clear as they usually are without that pressure.

We also know that pressure can kill you. We can have so much pressure on our hearts, physical or emotional, that we can have a heart attack and potentially die. The interesting thing about pressure is, when we are under it, what we are made up of is very important. Our makeup becomes crucial when we are under pressure, and that will determine how we're going to respond.

Think of pressure's effect on us this way: If I blew up a balloon all the way and tied it, and then I put that balloon on the ground and stepped on it, the pressure of my foot would make that balloon pop. But if I have a balloon and don't blow it all the way so there's still a little bit of room in there, then when I put my foot on that balloon, it merely expands and enlarges to displace the pressure.

If you try to handle your face-the-fire moments alone, your balloon will eventually pop when the pressure gets too heavy. When you're stressed to the max, there's finally no more of you left to handle life's next blow. On the other hand, if you live by faith and depend on God, He will provide you with a margin, a buffer that allows you to bend but not break.

So it's important to observe what happens when you face stressful situations. Because what's inside you will eventually reveal itself—you will either pop from fear or adjust by faith. You have to know what the Lord has called you to do, you have to see yourself there, and you have to be teachable in the midst of pressure and understand that when someone or something feels unbearable, it's time to run to your Father. It's time to stop and ask yourself, *Can I learn something in this uncomfortable place? Is God trying to teach me something? If I stop complaining for just a minute, is there an underlying lesson to be learned?*

Yes, life will not always be comfortable as you are finding your way from the dream to the fulfillment of it. But God promises that if you just pray and ask for help, He will do just that—help you! This was clear to me with the situation with Roy Hamilton, just as it was for Shadrach, Meshach, and Abednego when facing the furnace. God is always faithful when we face the fire and need His help. *Always.*

BABY STEPS

God can take *any* situation and make something beautiful come out of it. He uses the refiner's fire to burn away impurities and make us stronger. But we must be willing to trust Him and to learn from the process, even when it's scary and painful. I'm convinced this teachable characteristic is something our heavenly Father looks for in us as He guides us to the destiny He has for us. He knows we may become frightened or uncertain about where we're going and how we'll get there. But the Lord is so brilliant, He knew before we were born how He would take us there and help us to mature along the way, growing one step at a time.

Just like a baby learns to walk, it's one foot in front of the other—yes, baby steps—on the journey from dream to realization. Like that toddler learning how to walk, we will take a few steps and then fall down. It's all about balance and confidence. If we fall, we get back up and keep going. With every step we get a bit more confident, realizing, *Maybe I can actually do this—with God's help.* He empowers us to do what is impossible in our own ability. Greatness comes from our spark that turns into His flame.

So wherever you are, pick up your feet and keep walking! Learn to embrace the challenge, grow from the obstacles you encounter, and keep on trucking toward your dream. Just move forward. Make today the first day, and don't get stuck in yesterday. If you are reading this book and feeling pressure in your life right now, remember, often He allows these things to happen in order to propel us into our destiny. This means He is and was always in charge. You can face the fire knowing that He will bring you through it.

Remember, on the other side of your fear often lies your dream fulfilled.

SHIFTING RED MOMENTS TO GREEN TRIUMPHS

GO DEEPER

What situation are you presently facing that requires you to face your fears and step out in faith? What pressures are involved with this situation? How has your fear compounded the pressure you're facing? What's required for you to let go of trying to control this situation and invite God into it? Ask Him to show you how to face the current fire in your life.

GO FURTHER

Prayer is the surest way I know to overcome fear and transform it into faith. As you seek God's power to face the present fire in your life, I invite you to pray this prayer and make it your own:

Lord,

My mind is percolating and my heart is jumping with expectation. I know that situations and circumstances in my life have been addressed like never before. I thank You for planning out my destiny even before I was in my mother's womb.

Thank You that You did everything You needed to do concerning me even before I walked this earth.

Thank You, Lord, that I can take these new principles that I have learned and apply them to my life, knowing that I have what it takes to succeed. I now have new understanding concerning my dreams and future. I have new passion to run after everything You have for me in this life. Lord, my mind is encouraged.

I'm excited that when I next walk into my workplace, I will have extra pep in my step. Something has shifted in my heart because I know I was created to be there at this time. If not for the long term, my current job is a stepping-stone to the place You are moving me, the place that You have for me as long as I remain finely tuned and connected to You.

So I thank You for boldness, Lord God. I won't be afraid, because I know that You are my deliverer. I know You will put me on top, and You will build me up and plant me in Your perfect will.

*I know who I am, I know exactly what I am doing,
and, in turn, my future and where I am going is perfectly
orchestrated by You.
In Jesus' mighty name, amen.*

CHAPTER 3

RAISE A RED FLAG

REDEFINING RED WHEN YOU'RE DESPERATE

To hope means to be ready at every moment for that which is not yet born, and yet not become desperate if there is no birth in our lifetime.
—ERICH FROMM

After bouncing around in a variety of reporting and producing roles at local affiliates across the country, I landed in one of the major hubs of sports and entertainment reporting: Los Angeles, home of the Dodgers, Kings, Clippers, Sparks, and perhaps the city's best-known sports dynasty, the Lakers. As I soon discovered, nearly everyone calling themselves a resident of Los Angeles had at least a few items of yellow and purple in their closets. Rather than joining them, I remained committed to being an unbiased professional. But as I soon discovered while interviewing one of their opponents, the Utah Jazz, losing teams don't see it that way.

The NBA season was almost over, and I was part of an on-air team assigned to cover the game between the Lakers and the Jazz. While this was a regular-season game, it would likely determine playoff chances, and everyone's anticipation was off the charts. Fans, coaches, players, and even reporters—we were all excited to see a great battle on the court.

The game was a good one, and the Lakers increased their playoff chances by pulling out a win; however, my assignment was to interview players on the Jazz, whether they won or lost that night. With sports, you always have winners and losers, and that night, the Jazz was the latter of the two. Nevertheless, I trusted them to be as professional as I intended to be, grateful simply to be doing jobs we loved.

Little did I know, however, I was about to face an unexpected obstacle that would force me to change the way I did my job. But God did.

THE NAKED TRUTH

At the conclusion of the game, I made my way down the tunnel and into the waiting area outside the visiting team's locker room. Almost a dozen other media professionals surrounded me, and we waited and waited . . . and waited some more. After a half hour had passed, we realized something was out of the norm.

The losing team never likes to rush to the post-game press conference and interviews, but this was something else.

What we didn't know until later was that they were so upset and angry over the game, they didn't want to answer the uncomfortable questions they'd get after a loss. Basically, they didn't want to be bothered with the media. So in this case they decided to protest in an unconventional way. Yep, they simply said in unspoken terms, "Let's just not rush to put our clothes on." Their hopes were that reporters would leave, no questions would be asked, and they could just get out of there.

Let's be honest. When any of us loses, the last thing we want is to talk about it in public, right? While I understood how they felt, I also knew part of being a professional at this level was doing hard things that were part of your job—including talking to the media after the game. And that's why I was there—to do my job.

Of course, at the time we reporters had no idea they were doing this. It was only as we were finally cleared to go into the locker room, well over an hour after the game had ended, that we began to realize what the team was doing. Relieved to finally get on with doing my job, I walked in and couldn't believe what I saw. In fact, what I saw caused me to immediately look straight up at the ceiling! Not because there was some interesting mural up there, but because several guys in the room were still, well, let's just say they were still in the dressing stage.

Looking up and using my peripheral vision to guide my steps, I asked another reporter, "Uh, has anybody seen . . . ?" But my voice faded away as I lost my concentration from all the distraction—not to mention the focus required to keep my head above it all! I just couldn't function in such an environment when all my energy was being spent on not looking at the team members I was supposed to be intervieing.

Amid the smell of sweat, Icy Hot, and designer cologne, the tension was so combustible it felt like any little comment or wrong question might cause the room to explode. Yes, I was in the losing team's locker room, which is always a bit stressful. And they were really not in the mood to talk. And they'd decided to take their sweet time putting their clothes on. As many locker rooms as I had been in over the years, this was most certainly a first for me, and I didn't like it at all. Their choices were affecting me doing my job proficiently. I was not the only reporter who seemed extremely uncomfortable, but I also felt paralyzed in terms of getting my job done. This was awkward and just wrong on so many levels!

As I crept around trying to remain professional in this ridiculous environment, I prayed, "Lord, You're going to have to help me because I'm way out of my element here! I'm uncomfortable and I need You to help me. Please, Lord, now!" As my neck began to ache from looking up for so long, a veteran reporter came in, looked around the locker room, and headed straight for me—probably because of my red face and strained neck.

He pulled me aside and said, "Elictia, let me tell you something, because you are so good, and I can see that you are a little off your game tonight—and rightfully so. You're not the only one who's uncomfortable. I am just as uncomfortable as you are—I'm a man, and I'm still uncomfortable. But you get back in there. You kick butt, just the way I see you do week in and week out. If they don't want to put any clothes on, that's their choice and their problem. You let them know you are not deterred—or at least pretend like you're not bothered. Let them know that if they want to let it all hang out, okay, but you're a reporter and you're still going to ask questions and do your job."

Speechless, I soaked in his words. He was absolutely right! His wisdom was straightforward but life changing. His experience, born of almost five decades in broadcasting, spoke directly to my discomfort and insecurity. Like peanut butter to my jelly, his salty advice was the perfect reinforcement to my too-sweet demeanor. In a matter of moments, his words would forever affect my ability to do my job in any situation, comfortable or uncomfortable.

With newfound resolve and determination, I did what my colleague suggested and headed for the player I had been looking for this whole time. I looked him in the eye and said, "Okay, so here we go!" He looked back at me with his best poker face. "And by the way," I added, "can you get another towel and cover up some more?"

He looked at me a bit unnerved but proceeded to find his towel and do just as I requested. And from that day forward, I was more respected than ever because I let players know they didn't get to dictate how interviews went. I was there to do my job and do it well, whether they were clothed or not!

DESPERATE MEASURES

The outcome was positive only because of one crucial thing: in a crisis moment I was dependent on God and His provision. I will always treasure that wise, kind, and experienced man who taught me something invaluable in just a couple of sentences. I couldn't control what others did. At best, I could only influence them, like asking that player to cover up. But I could control the kind of job I did by keeping faith in God and what He had called me to do.

There's one caveat: I played a role in this moment as well. Yep, I had to be teachable and flexible in a stressful moment in my life. I had to choose how *I* would respond. Which sounds easier to do after the fact. In the moment, we just want things to be the way we want them to be, the way we expected them to be. As a result, our response to difficult situations varies like the waves hitting the shore. Just as the tide is often regular and even, sometimes we know how we will respond when life gets hectic, and other times we are just as shocked as those around us when storms come and life comes crashing down on us.

Stop for a moment and think about the various ways you have responded when life has thrown you a curve ball. Did you ask God for help? Were you flexible and teachable? Were you open to learn how you could rectify the situation or did you shut down and refuse to keep going? Your response in crisis situations will often determine the outcome. Perhaps this is a perfect place to lean on God's Word and see how He encourages us to respond. We're told, "Whoever disregards discipline comes to poverty and shame, but whoever heeds correction is honored" (Prov. 13:18).

Ouch! Yes, Scripture can be hard to swallow especially when we think we know it all—at least for me it is. Finding your way through this life and heading to your destiny of divine purpose must include red-flag moments. Moments of unexpected challenges and annoying obstacles. Moments of God-given guidance and constructive criticism.

And it's not just a matter of obedience and trusting God—He promises us that those who accept times of correction will be honored. Obstacles are not there to stop you but to unlock your potential. Correction means you're refining your route in the right direction. Depending on God means you can't do something yourself—and this is good, because if we could do everything ourselves, we might mistakenly think we didn't need God!

While correction may not always feel good, the great thing is, God will never leave you to sink. Your process is never one you have to go through alone. Consult with Him, and He will gladly help. I was so out of sorts in that locker room that all I could do was ask Him to help me; and because He is ever faithful, He did just that. He sent a veteran reporter, someone I recognized and respected, to teach me something in the form of correcting my thoughts and guiding my response to the situation.

Perhaps the old saying is true: desperate times call for desperate measures.

And the most desperate measure of all is prayer.

HOW DESPERATION BECOMES DETERMINATION

Desperation doesn't just happen when we encounter unexpected obstacles, like the one I experienced in the locker room that night. True desperation often runs much deeper and lasts longer. When you're really desperate, you long for God to do something—to provide, to resolve, to heal, to comfort, to guide—that you cannot do yourself. In fact, the source of your desperation may seem impossible by human standards. This kind of desperation creates intensity and fervor that can either drive you crazy or drive you to the Lord.

One of my heroes from the Old Testament is a woman forced to her knees in prayer time and time again as she begged God to give her the desire of her heart. Like so many women before and after her, Hannah yearned to have a child, a baby boy, who would complete her family and delight her husband. Let's take a look at the depth of her struggles:

> In her deep anguish Hannah prayed to the LORD, weeping bitterly. . . .
>
> As she kept on praying to the LORD, Eli observed her mouth. Hannah was praying in her heart, and her lips were moving but her voice was not heard. Eli thought she was drunk and said to her, "How long are you going to stay drunk? Put away your wine."
>
> "Not so, my lord," Hannah replied, "I am a woman who is deeply troubled. I have not been drinking wine or beer; I was pouring out my soul to the LORD. Do not take your servant for a wicked woman; I have been praying here out of my great anguish and grief."
>
> Eli answered, "Go in peace, and may the God of Israel grant you what you have asked of him." (1 Sam. 1:10, 12–17)

Can you imagine if your pastor heard you mumbling the same prayer over and over again to the point where he or she asked if you were *drunk*? Now that's desperate, my friend! Part of the backstory of Hannah's request involves her husband Elkanah's other wife—yes, polygamy was part of the culture at that time. This other woman wed to Elkanah apparently managed to become pregnant with no difficulty. But we're told Elkanah loved Hannah (1 Sam. 1:5) and always gave her a double portion of the meat he brought home. The other wife became jealous and taunted Hannah. She constantly reminded her that she had produced no children for her husband.

But Hannah's determination only strengthened as her rival kept insulting her. So Hannah refused to eat, sleep, or do anything except plead before God for the child she longed to have. I imagine she would go to the Lord's house and pray as fervently and passionately as she knew how, crying out, "I will do anything for You, Lord—please, just let me have a son." Even more, she decided that if God gave her this child she so desperately wanted, Hannah would give him back to God. She would dedicate her son to serving the Lord by letting him be raised in the temple and trained for the priesthood. Day after day, week after week, Hannah must have prayed and prayed, asking over and over for God to hear her heart's request.

Then one day she was there in the temple praying as the sun began going down. Can you imagine how long that poor woman must have been there? Just then, the old priest, Eli, showed up and began silently watching her. Maybe she even saw him, but ignored him as she went on with her deep, heartfelt prayers before the throne of God. Maybe Eli even gave Hannah a funny look and wondered what was wrong with her. Which might explain how he came to ask her if she was drunk.

And that's when she shared her burden with the old priest and explained why her eyes were so red and her speech so broken. Seeing this distraught woman's tear-streaked face and hearing her desperate explanation, Eli accepted her answer and blessed her, joining her request with his for God to grant her desire. Hannah thanked him and left, perhaps eager to tell her husband that the temple priest had actually thought she was drunk!

Out of the red flag of Hannah's desperation came the power of surrendering to God's will. I love the way she refused to give up hope and just kept praying, trusting, and asking God. Too often, we're tempted to give up—on ourselves, on our dreams, on God— when we encounter an obstacle we don't know how to move. But that's the entire point of needing God. As Jesus Himself once explained to His disciples, "With man this is impossible, but with God all things are possible" (Matt. 19:26).

Hannah's story has a Hallmark-happy ending, but even if it hadn't, she had still learned to depend on God in the midst of her desperation. After she returned home, by the next day her appetite had returned and she realized how hungry she was. After eating and regaining her strength, she also experienced a deepening of her faith, a trust in God to provide her with a son. And sure enough, she and Elkanah conceived a son born nine months later, Samuel, whom they dedicated to serving God. And the baby's name, Samuel, means "God heard me."

Hannah's story remains incredibly relevant to us as we consider our own longings and how we handle them. And it's not just because her story has a happy ending, with her getting what she wanted. The thing we must always remember is that Hannah was faithful not knowing whether her heart's desire would ever come to pass. Based on all the months when her dream clearly did not come true, Hannah refused to give up. She reminds us that when we're desperate, we must choose to seek God.

Perhaps our starting point is simply naming what we want. Too often, we get so stressed by all the busyness of working, shopping, cooking, cleaning, and dropping the kids off and starting all over again, that we may not even be sure of what we want. What are you presently longing for in your life?

Can you relate to Hannah's brand of longing for something special and significant in your life? Like her, you may long to have children and may have struggled with being able to conceive. Maybe you desire a spouse and have not found a lasting partner to whom you can commit the rest of your life. It might be your college degree or a certain job in a particular field of work. You might want to launch your own business or pursue early retirement or start a new ministry.

Each and every one of us has a dream, something we believe is part of our destiny, but which doesn't always seem to follow our timetable and expectations. And the older we get, the harder it likely becomes to trust that this longing will ever be fulfilled. Are you willing to remain faithful and obedient to God regardless of whether He gives you this desire?

Just consider how long Hannah waited and all she endured from the mean-spirited woman to whom Hannah's husband was also wed. Hannah certainly must have known how hard it is to want something so badly that you ache to have it. To want it so very much and then to watch your chances growing slimmer and further away. And then to make it worse, watching others get what you want with ease, maybe without even seeming to try, care, or appreciate what they're given.

Hannah reminds us that our longings and expectations can make our lives more difficult. But they can also make our faith stronger and our relationship with God closer. When we face desperate situations, we often realize that faith is our only resource.

SHIFTING RED MOMENTS
TO GREEN TRIUMPHS

GO DEEPER

What is your expectation for today? What is the focus of your current desperation? What are you hoping to see God do in your life? Are you living out of what you know to be true about God or out of your own way of controlling things in your life? What do you need to surrender before God in order to overcome your desperation and transform it to dedication to Him?

GO FURTHER

After reflecting and perhaps praying about your answers to the previous questions, take a few moments and write out your thoughts. Consider areas of desperation that you have been afraid to unlock because of how painful they might be—healing for past sins, secret addictions, shameful abuse. What is the deepest longing of your heart right now for this deep, desperate part of you? How long have you been praying and seeking healing for this area? Where has God met you in the midst of this longing in the past? How do you want Him to meet you in it now? After writing out your responses, spend a few minutes in prayer, thanking God for what He's done and for what He's about to do in your life.

CHAPTER 4

DETOURS AND NEW DIRECTIONS

REDEFINING RED WHEN YOU'RE LOST

*If you don't get lost, there's a chance
you may never be found.*

—Anonymous

What on earth? I thought as I rubbed my eyes, weary from reading too many scripts in the newsroom. "Can that really be . . . ?" Walking into the station and standing only a few feet away from me was one of the greatest, most iconic people in the history of broadcast journalism. He set a standard for excellence, integrity, and on-air performance that remains the highest in the field. His name was Walter Cronkite.

You may be too young to remember him, but Mr. Cronkite helped launch the *CBS Evening News* and put television news coverage on the map. Best known as "the most trusted man in America" for several decades, he covered every major event during the turbulent 1960s and '70s: the assassinations of President Kennedy as well as Dr. King, the war in Vietnam, the *Apollo* moon landing, Watergate, and the Iran hostage crisis, among others.

His unflappable, deep baritone voice delivered the news with a kind of strength, empathy, and gravitas that assured viewers that despite all the terrible things happening in the world, life would go on. Mr. Cronkite ended each broadcast with his own catchphrase, "And that's the way it is . . ." followed by that day's date. I had grown up watching him, and in my small, finite mind, he wasn't just a newsman; he *was* the news!

And, yes, it really was him—pinch me!—right there on a normal Tuesday afternoon in my station's newsroom, a CBS affiliate in Anchorage, Alaska. My coworkers and I had been preparing for our 5:00 and 6:00 p.m. newscasts when this legend walked in, so unassuming and matter-of-fact. But our hustle and bustle abruptly stopped when he walked through the door.

PRIMARY SOURCE

It was surreal to see the man who virtually defined what a television news anchor should be standing and talking to our news director—only a finger's touch away from me! I couldn't imagine what he was doing here, and my teammates, all just as green and inexperienced as I was, were as in awe of him as I was. Our initial silence gave way to the buzz of whispered questions as we unconsciously gathered in a circle around him and our director. Why was he here? How long would he be here? Did we get to talk to him? Would he be staying for the newscast? And who was the lady with him? So many questions.

Sensing we were spinning out of control, our news director silenced us by saying, "Mr. Cronkite and his wife, Betsy, are on vacation here in Anchorage and decided to drop by the local CBS station." Aha. Finally it made sense. After all, we were in one of the most unique and beautiful states in the country, and who doesn't have Alaska on their bucket list! Retired for many years, Mr. Cronkite embodied the truth, "once a journalist, always a journalist," and he couldn't resist spontaneously dropping by the station.

So we quickly gave him the unimpressive tour of our little station. Once formalities were over and our initial questions had been answered, I probably wasn't the only one who felt a little starstruck and unsure of what to say. How do you have a conversation with a larger-than-life personal hero in your field? But Mr. Cronkite made it so easy and natural for us, smiling and commenting on the way our newsroom was set up or asking about what we were working on for that night's broadcasts.

It was so easy to feel his paternal nature exuding from each word he spoke. With his white hair, bushy eyebrows, mustache, and rosy cheeks, he was like everybody's grandpa, wise and kind, calm and aware of secrets we all wanted to know. As a young broadcast journalist climbing the ladder from station to station, I was eager to sit at his feet and listen to his wealth of wisdom and, frankly, *anything* he wanted to say.

Thinking back now, I don't even know how long we chatted,

and at that time it didn't matter; we learned a lifetime of tips from one of the best. Nothing over the top, no unheard-of revelations, just simple wisdom to hydrate our dreams and help us along the journey, small tidbits that would shape my future and help me understand my past. Namely, dream big, work hard, and *never* give up. "Keep dreaming," he said, "but remember, success requires passion and *endurance*."

Finally, he thanked us for allowing them to drop in on us, and then I felt like the luckiest girl in the world as I got to take pictures with him and then with him and his wife. And with that they were gone.

VALLEY OF THE SHADOW

When I recall that afternoon spent with Walter Cronkite, I'm amazed at the impact it had. I've never forgotten his motto because it's one I've always tried to live by, both as a journalist and as a person, especially when life gets crazy and I feel like giving up. One of those seasons had occurred a few years before meeting Mr. Cronkite when I faced some major decisions about which direction my life would take.

Working for FOX Sports, I knew in a professional sense I had finally arrived, at least in my little mind, anyway. I was based in Seattle, my hometown, covering teams I grew up watching: the Seahawks, Mariners, and Sonics. It was a dream come true. I lived in beautiful digs on Lake Washington, drove a new SUV, and loved my job in the rocking-and-rolling world of professional sports. My life was *so* good.

Until it wasn't.

One day at work the "suits" began calling my coworkers into their offices and laying them off. It was terrifying. I had no idea if I would be safe or if I would be the next to be called. Two days went by, and I watched so many people I cared about and enjoyed working with box up their belongings and say a quick, tearful goodbye. Then it was my turn to be called into the corporate office, and I knew it was not good news.

They said they had tried to do everything they could; they even maneuvered some people so they didn't have to let me go. But honestly, I couldn't even hear the words they were saying. It was like hearing Charlie Brown's teacher, "*Womp, womp womp . . .*" Unfortunately nothing they could say mattered. If you've been through this experience, then I'll bet you agree. There's nothing anyone can say to ease the situation. But I did manage to depart on a gracious note despite how I felt. Mustering every ounce of strength I had, I remember saying, "Thank you. It's been wonderful working for FOX, and I learned so much."

So there I was in a completely horrific situation. In the television industry, other stations, programs, and networks only want to hire you when you have a job. It's most difficult to get a job when you don't have a job. And of course I hadn't been applying any place because I had a job, a good one that I enjoyed very much. I thought there was no reason to be sending tapes out and applying elsewhere.

Fortunately I had saved my money, so I didn't panic right away. I could only hope this jobless season would pass by quickly. All was well as the first, second, third, and fourth months passed. By the fifth month my agent had to assure me not to worry. But I was getting worried. After all, I had a mortgage, a car payment, and other monthly bills. So I tried to be frugal as I looked for another job and processed the disappointment that accompanied my new lack of direction.

It wasn't easy, but I wanted to believe God still knew what He was doing. Maybe there was an even better job out there. Maybe He had something more directly related to serving His kingdom waiting for me. I couldn't know, but I had to keep hoping and keep trying. This became my definition of endurance, especially after months of walking through hard times. Endurance means staying the course when all you want to do is give up. Endurance requires the faith to follow God and find a new way forward when you feel lost.

FAITH FORWARD

During this time I became even closer to another of my personal heroes, a champion of endurance named Ruth. When I lost my job, Ruth's story reminded me to look within myself and find the strength to trust God and persevere, even when I felt lost and couldn't see where I was going. Let's consider her story, as told in the Old Testament book of Ruth, and how it can continue to provide a compass of hope in our Father's faithfulness.

Ruth's story actually begins with her in-laws, Naomi and Elimelech, who had moved across the border from Judah. Considering our country's recent recession and ongoing economic turbulence, it's easy to understand why a family would need to leave home in search of work and a new life elsewhere. For Naomi and Elimelech, this change meant leaving behind their struggle in

Bethlehem and starting over in the foreign land of Moab. It was a big risk, and for a while it must have felt like it paid off. Even with the unexpected death of her husband, Naomi could take comfort that her two adult sons remained nearby after marrying local young women.

Ten years went by, and just when Naomi finally started enjoying her life again, the unthinkable happened. This mother lost not one but *both* of her loving sons. Scripture doesn't tell us how they died or why, only that they both perished around the same time. No mother ever wants to consider outliving her babies, even when they're adults. Naomi had to be crushed. She had lost her husband and both sons in just a little more than a decade, all since coming to a place that must have started to feel unbearable after all the pain she'd experienced there. She must have felt totally lost, unable to remain in Moab, even after God had apparently led her family there.

So Naomi decided to move back to her hometown, probably not expecting that her two daughters-in-law, Orpah and Ruth, would want to go with her. But they did. As sweet as their willingness to go with her was, though, Naomi couldn't allow these young women to leave their homeland and start over in an unfamiliar place.

> Then Naomi said to her two daughters-in-law, "Go back, each of you, to your mother's home. May the LORD show you kindness, as you have shown kindness to your dead husbands and to me. May the LORD grant that each of you will find rest in the home of another husband . . ."
>
> At this they wept aloud again. Then Orpah kissed her mother-in-law goodbye, but Ruth clung to her. (Ruth 1:8–14)

It was a confusing and painful time, and Naomi gave her daughters-in-law the perfect out. She didn't want them to endure the same kind of suffering and hardship that she knew she would likely face for the rest of her life. Naomi even assumed the Lord's hand had turned against her because of her hard circumstances, and she didn't want her sons' wives to be caught up in the same unexpected, devastating detour.

And while Orpah took the opportunity to turn around and go back to Moab, Ruth chose a different path. While Orpah saw a time to stop, Ruth saw a time to go. Why? Because she loved her mother-in-law and couldn't bear to abandon her to face the world alone. Ruth, unfamiliar with the God of her deceased husband and his family, nonetheless displayed faith in the Lord's goodness.

When we feel lost and confused by unexpected events or an unbearable loss, we must remember Ruth's example of endurance. She loved others as well as God with a depth of commitment that's rare. Not only was she unwilling to abandon her beloved mother-in-law, but Ruth somehow found the courage to keep going toward the destiny God had for them. She was willing to trust that God had not brought them together that far to leave them in an impossible situation.

And if you know the rest of Ruth's story, you of course know that God did indeed provide for her and Naomi's well-being in the most dramatic way—their kinsman redeemer back in Bethlehem, Boaz, a wealthy landowner, took care of them and came to love and marry Ruth. The happy ending gets even more dramatic! Boaz and Ruth had a son named Obed, who became the father of Jesse, who was the father of King David, the shepherd boy anointed by God to be Israel's king.

And it doesn't end there, of course, because David's family tree leads directly to the manger, to God's Son, Jesus. In fact, Ruth's name is listed in the genealogy of Christ in the New Testament, a feat in itself since mothers' names were rarely listed. The story of Ruth reminds us that when our expectations go off the tracks, we must trust God to guide us and lead us to our ultimate destination. He always has a plan.

A TEST OF ENDURANCE

It can be hard to trust God with His plan when nothing seems to be going our way. Like Ruth and Naomi, we will inevitably have our endurance tested. After losing my job, for the first time ever, I could not pay my car insurance. At this point I began to really tell God how I was feeling, and I have to admit I was a bit upset, perhaps like our girl Naomi leaving Moab. Still I kept trusting God to provide and to turn things around. I endured because I knew that how I responded to these setbacks would determine what happened next.

In this season of my life I was being stretched to the core of who I was. And the one question I kept asking myself was, would I have the resilience I needed to bounce back? You see, all the conveniences in my life were no longer easily attained. I was being broken and stripped of everything I knew. Was this the "rock bottom" I had only heard people talk about? If so, I had crashed right down into it. What was once the norm in my life was no longer the norm.

And right when I couldn't imagine my circumstances getting any worse, they did! It was Thanksgiving night, and my sister and I were driving home after a lovely time with family and friends when a car came out of nowhere and hit me. The driver had run a red light turning left through an intersection. Remember how I had let my car insurance lapse? Not good.

You can only imagine how much I was shaking. No job, no insurance, and now a car that was embarrassing to drive. That's right; when you have duct tape holding your bumper on, you can't roll your driver's-side window down, and there is no side mirror on your car, it's officially embarrassing to drive! Try going to a drive-through with a window that won't roll down— you have to pull up and open your door!

There I was, a former FOX Sports news reporter, a broadcast professional on the fast track, suddenly forced to roll along with dangling parts and duct tape on her car. Now, I realize in the scope of world hunger, persecution of believers, and the many terrible crises around the globe my troubles were light, but in the moment they overwhelmed me.

And my pride got in the way. In my younger days, I would have just shrugged, taken the bus, and thought nothing about it. Or I could have asked my parents for help, but every time I considered it, I'd think, *No, you're a grown woman! You can't go calling Mom and Dad!* So for the time being, I kept driving my wrecked car around, always trying to park where the good side was showing.

Nevertheless, I kept going, kept enduring. Six months passed without a job, then seven, then eight. I was honestly starting to panic. I remember praying, "Lord, what's going on? Are You up there on Your throne so high You can't even hear me? Anybody there? Have You seen my car lately? It's not doing so well. And my landlord has knocked on my door again for rent, and while he's gracious, his patience is running out. Please, Lord, I need help!"

WHO'S HOLDING YOUR LADDER?

The only way I survived that brutal season in my life after the layoff (and I did survive—more on that in the next chapter) was by trusting God and learning to rely on other people. When you feel lost, you inevitably feel alone and may be tempted to withdraw and isolate yourself even more. Surrounding yourself with people who are going in the same direction spiritually is a critical aspect of achieving your God-appointed destiny.

Mitch, my boss at my old job down in Hattiesburg, Mississippi, remains one of the most positive, influential encouragers I've ever had. To this day he will call and say, "Elictia Hart, how you doin'?" I love to hear his strong Southern accent. I smile when I think about all I learned from him, including how to get through setbacks.

And it wasn't just that time I shared with you earlier when I was doing the live broadcast in the stormy weather. Mitch was always teaching and leading in everything we did. It was just his nature. I recall once at a Friday night football game, an on-field incident became a teaching moment.

We were going about our normal duties and getting ready to shoot the football game when Mitch said, "Do you see what's happening right there?" I looked over and saw the coach and a player going at it. Mitch said, "Right now, that young man right there has just stepped out of covenant with his coach. He is not respecting the authority to which he has submitted by wearing that uniform." We had so many moments like that when Mitch was not only making a better journalist out of me but teaching me how to be a woman of God.

At this low point of my life, I remembered people like Mitch and appreciated their wisdom, counsel, and encouragement more than ever. I felt like I had been knocked off my corporate climb up the ladder of success, but people like Mitch helped me get back on my feet and get back on that ladder.

Where you are going and what the Lord has called you to do is specific to you. Not everyone can help guide you because not everyone has the wisdom or insight to help you arrive at this destination. So, just as you have to surround yourself with people who are going where you are going, you also have to be careful who you are following or listening to.

Think of a baby taking his or her first steps. As a mom, when my twins were growing into toddlers and learning to walk, I would say, "Come on, you can do it. I've got you!" I'd keep my hands stretched out ready to catch them, support them, and cheer them on. Let's take this analogy up a notch and go vertical. As you climb the ladder of where God is taking you, imagine the people you want holding it steady for you.

So the person holding your ladder is critical. Ruth refused to leave Naomi during her darkest days and remained committed to helping her climb to the next rung. Later, once they had returned to Bethlehem, Naomi returned the favor and counseled Ruth on her relationship with Boaz. David had Jonathan. Paul had Barnabas and Timothy. The people we allow into our lives can make a huge difference when we're struggling and feeling lost.

From my experience, the ladder-holders should be people who have done some climbing themselves so they can share what they've learned from their experience. You want them to be people who have climbed the ladder themselves so they can give you tips to make your climb smooth. You want them to be people who want to see you succeed, people who believe in you, and people who are not afraid to correct you.

What I'm saying is, not everyone can hold your ladder. In fact, only certain people can and should hold your ladder in certain seasons of your life. The ladder that Mitch held got me to a certain point. He had knowledge and expertise and was willing to boost me higher with his help.

Someone else who comes to mind is Kevin Frazier, who worked with me at FOX Sports and went on to coanchor *Entertainment Tonight*. He worked at ESPN and many different places, but there was a period of time when he held my ladder. I could call him, ask him questions, and get direction for my career because he was where I was going.

Mitch and Kevin are just two of the many who have guided me and held my ladder along the way. They have been a crucial part of my journey. You can never underestimate the importance of being led by someone who has been there and can help you find your way.

FINDING YOUR WAY

When you find yourself in difficult situations that you'd rather not face, you have to persevere and take it day by day, hour by hour. When you feel lost, life becomes an endurance test, requiring a blend of resilience and patience that only comes from within. I think of it as "purposed" patience, the kind when you have to choose to be patient, trust in God, and endure your present circumstances.

When we feel lost in the unexpected detours and derailments

of life, we must trust that God knows where we're going and how we'll get there. The all-knowing One, your Father in heaven, planned your life and knew what you would have to face. But He loves you and has your best interests at heart, even when you can't see what He's doing or why He's allowing certain events. This gives me a crazy peace!

So much of what we worry about is beyond our control, so worrying about it accomplishes absolutely nothing. On the other hand, we know with God that nothing is impossible, and nothing is beyond His control. Even when our lives feel out of control, we can relax knowing He's got everything taken care of. I love what King David wrote in one of his many songs of praise to God in the Psalms:

> GOD, investigate my life;
> > get all the facts firsthand.
> I'm an open book to you;
> > even from a distance, you know what I'm thinking.
> You know when I leave and when I get back;
> > I'm never out of your sight.
> You know everything I'm going to say
> > before I start the first sentence.
> I look behind me and you're there,
> > then up ahead and you're there, too—
> > your reassuring presence, coming and going.
> > > (PS. 139:1–5 THE MESSAGE)

This psalm reminds us that God holds the map for our life's journey as well as the fuel. Because He created us, we would be wise to align our desires with Him and His plans for our lives.

We just have to plug into the One who has the ultimate GPS for our lives, following His guidance and direction to our divinely anointed destination.

Or, instead of a map, think of God's vision for your life as a blueprint. Created by architects and followed by builders to bring a house or building to life, blueprints provide a picture of both the parts and the whole. If you're on a construction site, it's not the carpenters, electricians, plumbers, and other crewmembers creating the vision of the finished structure and directing everyone else. No, it's the builder who unites all these direct players and their various contributions to create a beautifully constructed whole.

Similarly, God is our Master Builder who holds the blueprints for our lives and wants to empower us to live out our full potential. He sees what others, including ourselves, cannot always see. He knows what we can endure and wants us to grow and become stronger through our weaknesses. The apostle Paul said, "We are God's handiwork, created in Christ Jesus to do good works, which God prepared in advance for us to do" (Eph. 2:10). Since He knows what's next, what goes where, and how things all fit together, it's easy for Him to guide us. Don't you want someone who knows what's going on leading you? I sure do!

I love what Moses told the children of Israel as recorded in Deuteronomy. After nearly forty years of leading them out of Egypt and searching for their new home, Moses, at 121 years old, informed them he would no longer be the person leading them into the promised land. Instead, God had chosen Joshua to lead them. Knowing this transition and that what lay ahead could bring great fear to the people, the Lord reassured them through Moses that their enemies were already defeated and all was well.

How was this possible? Because God had the blueprint. He

knew Israel would face opposition from their enemies, leaving them anxious and afraid. This transfer of power was a clear reminder to them that God alone held the blueprints of their lives and that He would be there to guide them as well as give them courage to face whatever obstacles they encountered. Moses said, "Be strong and courageous! Do not be afraid and do not panic before them. For the LORD your God will personally go ahead of you. He will neither fail you nor abandon you" (Deut. 31:6 NLT).

Knowing God holds the blueprints of our lives gives us encouragement when things seem difficult. We can remember who we are and whose we are and keep walking by faith even when the path goes dark. We are His children, His handiwork, and more precious than rubies! We are fearfully and wonderfully made, created in His image and empowered by His Holy Spirit. Our circumstances may change, but these timeless truths remain the same. God is the same yesterday, today, and tomorrow as promised in His Word (Heb. 13:8). No matter how lost you may feel, He will show you the way.

SHIFTING RED MOMENTS TO GREEN TRIUMPHS

GO DEEPER

What's the hardest situation you've had to face in your life so far? How did it humble you or force you to depend on God? What did you learn from it? How did going through this detour allow you to trust God more the next time circumstances didn't go as planned?

GO FURTHER

Everyone needs people who will hold their ladders for them, especially when we fall and need help getting up and back on the ladder. Who's holding your ladder? Or who *could* or should hold your ladder? Do you have a mentor in your life who is giving you a boost when needed? If so, make an appointment with that person this week for lunch or a conversation over coffee. If you don't have someone holding your ladder right now, spend some extra time in prayer and ask God to provide the right person in His timing who can help lift you up to the next level.

CHAPTER 5

SACRIFICING YOUR ISAAC

REDEFINING RED WHEN YOU'RE STUCK

Hope deferred makes the heart sick; but when dreams come true at last, there is life and joy.

—PROVERBS 13:12 (TLB)

*H*ow did this happen? *I asked myself as I got out of my car. How did I get to this point?*

I took a few steps and pulled my raincoat tighter to ward off the chilly mist hovering in the grey skies around me. The air smelled like a mixture of diesel and briny saltwater from the nearby harbor. It was early, yet commuters and pedestrians already clogged the streets and sidewalks.

It just doesn't make sense, I thought to myself. *I've worked for some of the finest places in the broadcasting industry. National networks and global franchises. I've interviewed sports legends like Shaquille O'Neal and Tiger Woods, Kobe Bryant and Steve McNair. And now I'm about to walk into a temp agency and take any job they've got for me.*

I pushed away the hurt and put on my game face. It was hard enough to get up early, shower, pick out a professional-looking ensemble—nothing too flashy but something that still had style, do my makeup and hair, and drive to downtown Seattle. I didn't want to fall apart emotionally on top of all I had done to drag myself down here.

The agency was located on the top floor of a glass-and-brick office building overlooking a strip mall, a warehouse, and several other taller buildings. I followed the sign and climbed the stairs, careful not to trip in my heels. Had it really been that long since I lost my job that I couldn't even walk in heels?

"Hello. Do we have you in our system? Did you call ahead?" asked an older lady sitting at the receptionist's desk.

I tried to smile and said, "No, I'm not in your system yet, and yes, I made an appointment yesterday."

"Great," she said, distracted by someone who had just entered behind me. "Sign your name here and someone will be with you shortly."

I did as instructed, nodded, took off my raincoat, and found a seat in the lobby waiting area. The place looked shabby and felt as tired as my spirit. Sighing deeply and saying a prayer, I pulled out the file folder with copies of my résumé and looked over it one more time. Hard to believe the former golden girl had lost her shine.

"Elictia?" A tall, slender woman with short, brown hair smiled and motioned for me to follow her. We sat in a small cubicle not far from the receptionist, and I handed over my résumé as we made polite small talk. As she scanned the sheet of crisp, white linen-stock paper, her face said it all. She looked across at me sympathetically and said, "Wow, *Entertainment Tonight*, ESPN, FOX—you're quite accomplished. You do realize we don't handle television jobs here, don't you?" She smiled at me as if assessing whether I was naive or just desperate.

"Yes, I realize that." I returned her smile as confidently as I could manage.

From there, we went through a normal interview process, and she described some of the entry-level administrative positions they had available. I indicated my willingness to accept any assignment—filing, typing, note taking—anything that would provide a paycheck. She thanked me and I was on my way.

The whole thing only took about twenty minutes, but I felt like years had passed. I had just done something I never imagined doing. I was no longer a broadcast professional. I was a temp.

COPY THAT

As I left the temp agency and walked back to my car, I began talking to my heavenly Father. You see, I knew He was working on my heart. He was shedding light on my pride and humbling me, all in love. It felt like much the same thing my earthly father used to do, gently teaching me through life experiences.

The past months had been some of the hardest in my life,

filled with uncertainty and fear, with anxiety and worry about when my career would resume. After I lost my job, I knew it would be a dry season for a while, but when leads became dead ends week after week, I began to feel stuck. While I knew the job drought had to end sometime, many days I found my faith stretched to the breaking point.

As lonely as I felt, I knew I wasn't walking the road alone. Despite my fears about the future, I trusted the Lord was leading me every step of the way. In the midst of my ego-crushing interview with the temp agency, I believed God would provide.

And He did. The next day the lady from the temp agency called and said one of the Google subsidiaries had a position. I accepted it immediately and said I could begin the next day. When I arrived at Google the next morning, I had once again taken great care with my appearance; I was nicely dressed in a suit and prepared to work hard. I was determined to get through this humbling situation as positively as possible.

After checking in and being directed to a department down the hall, I was greeted by a man who clearly looked surprised that I was the temp. Me, well, I was just happy to be going to work! Even when I was informed of my job for the next two weeks: photocopying. Yep, you read that right. I photocopied, I took staples out, I did the jobs that no one in that company wanted to do. So much that they had to have a temp—me—come in and do it.

As I photocopied, I soon realized the other employees didn't know I existed. They didn't speak to me, offer to help me, or really even acknowledge me. In fact, they were pretty much rude to me. I felt invisible, and it was a horrible feeling. Still I tried to keep a positive attitude and a pleasant expression on my face.

And I photocopied, and I photocopied. And then I photocopied some more!

But here's the awesome thing: I was not photocopying alone. God began to speak to my heart while I stood between my best friends, Xerox 1 and Xerox 2. He asked me, *Do you realize that you were sometimes rude to people along your journey? Do you remember when one of the production assistants asked you to help them? And do you remember how you treated them? Do you remember when you walked past that new reporter who came in so very green and frightened? And how irritated you were when she didn't have your scripts ready?*

Anyone walking by certainly wouldn't have noticed the distant look in my eyes. But my heart broke as I realized that I had been much the same as my new coworkers back in the good old days when I was such a big shot.

It was like God gently took my hand and led me to sit down with Him as He revealed some things inside my heart. The places in my heart that were ugly and not like Him. That were not loving and kind and gracious. Then He said to me, *I'm here to show you that every part is valuable. You're right where you're supposed to be right now. See, they need somebody to photocopy these papers. They do this once a year, and they need someone to do it because they can't complete their work if it's not done. Do your best and do it for Me—not just them.*

For the next ten days while I was photocopying, the grace of God was so strong that I felt I was doing the most important job in the building. Seriously, who knew photocopying could ever be so exhilarating? But God was working on my heart at that moment, and He graced me through it.

Again, it was almost like I wasn't even photocopying. I stood back and God showed and revealed things to me during this time as I began checking my heart, assessing my motives, and reflecting on the person I was. He was showing me areas where I needed to grow and treat others the way I wanted to be treated. He was revealing the value of having a loving heart—a heart that appreciates everyone for who they are. He was showing me all of humanity is important. Yes, everyone has different skill sets and knowledge, but every human being is precious. Every part contributes to the whole—and of course, God's Word makes this as clear as can be:

> As it is, there are many parts, but one body.
>
> The eye cannot say to the hand, "I don't need you!" And the head cannot say to the feet, "I don't need you!" On the contrary, those parts of the body that seem to be weaker are indispensable, and the parts that we think are less honorable we treat with special honor. And the parts that are unpresentable are treated with special modesty, while our presentable parts need no special treatment. But God has put the body together, giving greater honor to the parts that lacked it, so that there should be no division in the body, but that its parts should have equal concern for each other. If one part suffers, every part suffers with it; if one part is honored, every part rejoices with it.
>
> Now you are the body of Christ, and each one of you is a part of it. (1 Cor. 12:20–27)

Think of your body. Every part needs the next. Your feet can't work without your head, and your fingers need your hands in order to function. Every part is necessary and valuable, although each operates with different functions. Even though I wasn't doing what I wanted to be doing, I realized that I was just as valuable to God as when I had been a reporter for a global network.

I still mattered.

My Father still loved me as much as He ever had.

I wasn't alone.

I no longer felt stuck.

ETERNAL THINKING

By working at that temp-agency job where all I did was photocopy, I grew spiritually in leaps and bounds. All of a sudden everything in my life that had been dragging me down seemed trivial. It didn't matter that I had lost my job, it didn't matter that I was working for a temp agency, it didn't matter that I spent forty hours a week photocopying, and suddenly it didn't matter that my car was being held together by duct tape. Yes, imagine that! All those superficial surface details were fading in significance. Instead I was learning what it means to view life the way God sees it, to have what I call eternal thinking.

Eternal thinking allows you to control your response to things that happen in life. Situations and circumstances no longer affect you the way they once did. You no longer sweat the small stuff because you have such a clear view of the big eternal stuff. You realize these situations you are going through in life won't affect your eternal life. Stressing out about things—especially those beyond your control—only robs you of the joy, peace, and purpose you can enjoy if you shift perspectives.

My car having duct tape on it didn't affect my life long-term.

Working for a temp agency would never keep me from fulfilling the call God had already placed on my life. Not being able to afford the luxuries I had grown used to having was not a problem when I remembered how many huge blessings I had in my life: a family who loved me, friends who cared and encouraged me, a place to live, food to eat, and yes, a car to drive even if it was a little banged up.

As my thoughts, attitude, and perspective shifted, I was humbled beyond belief. I was humbled to the point of realizing every person and every creation are precious in God's sight. My life—all of it, even this painful season of feeling stuck—was wonderful and valuable. You see, something happens inside your heart when you're cut down like I was. As God spoke and convicted my heart, I had to decide if I was going to believe the Word of the Lord about what's true, or if I was going to believe the Feelings of Elictia!

I had to decide whether I was going to let God be God. I was stretched beyond myself during those weeks and months, but I grew more in that short, concentrated period of time than I have since. When God is cultivating your character and helping you grow beyond your limitations, it's not usually a fun process. Especially if you're a strong-willed person who likes being in control, like I am.

Here's what I realized from my time in that career desert. The high value I placed on my career made it difficult to relinquish when God wanted me to move on to new ventures. I had let it define me as a success instead of the mess I first felt without it. I had placed a high value on my appearance, my reputation in the industry, and my exclusive interviews—not to mention my new cars, nice things, and designer clothing.

Without realizing it, I had placed a high value on things more than people—and sometimes even more than God. But He loved me too much to leave me in that condition. God doesn't ask us to relinquish things to play with our minds or to upset us or to let us suffer just for the fun of it. No, He gives us the right to make our own choices and to face the consequences. This freedom of choice, my friend, is exactly what makes life so difficult.

Remember in the Bible when Abraham had a choice to make when it came to sacrificing his son Isaac? Such a request may seem unfathomable to us, but God was looking at Abraham's character. You have to believe it was not an easy road traveling up a mountain knowing you were going to sacrifice your son. You have to believe Abraham questioned God, was baffled by God, and didn't completely understand what God was doing in his life at that moment.

Sound familiar? Have you ever experienced events in your life that just didn't make sense? Lost your job? Someone you love betrayed your trust? A battle with cancer? Lost a child in a car accident or to an addiction? Every day people face devastating, unexpected losses that send them reeling to make sense of their lives.

When my life didn't make sense, I tried to keep going on my own power, but inside I was hurt, confused, and uncertain about why God would allow me to experience such a loss. Just as Abraham was likely doubtful, afraid, and upset, I was totally confused during this season in my life. Ultimately, Abraham pleased God because his plans were placed in God's hands. Abraham relinquished his own plans and wishes. His character pleased the Lord, and ultimately Abraham saw a ram in the bush, which God had provided so Isaac would not have to be sacrificed. Instead, the ram was the sacrifice.

While it wasn't the life of my child, I, too, had a choice to relinquish my plans. I had a choice, and that's why it was so hard: I had placed a high value on my own "Isaac." Because the value I'd placed on my career and all it provided was so high, it was very difficult for me to lay it down. Ultimately, I'm so grateful that my character was fine tuned in this season.

When I finally did get another TV job, had my car repaired, and caught up on some bills, more important, I also had a much closer relationship with my Creator! And I believe, just to show me I passed my test of sorts, I was offered not one, not two, but three jobs in the same week. Oh, yes—He was smiling on me! From no TV job to three offers in one week. This season of growth ended with a *huge* bang. Even today, sharing this story always gets me. He had a plan for me even through the storm.

Getting another job was just an added bonus on top of what the Lord had already given me. His love, compassion, and guidance during this incredible season of my life allowed me to have a renewed mind, causing me to think eternally and not just for the moment I was in. He got me unstuck and refocused me on what matters most.

TIME FOR A CHANGE

It took me a while, but I eventually realized how God was turning my terrible season into a triumphant opportunity to be closer to Him. I'm convinced that often when we feel stuck or encounter obstacles in our path, God has something He can teach us from the experience if we will let Him. But if we're only focused on our own pain, frustration, and uncertainty, we miss out on God's good stuff.

Change is tough for all of us, but especially for kids. For instance, my son, Micah, is one little guy who likes predictability. Like many of us, when things are not what he expects, he gets a bit off-kilter. Micah knows we have a routine at bedtime. We read a story out of a Bible devotional, then both his dad and I pray for him and his twin sister, Jemma. What's funny, though, is that even when it comes to the prayer, Micah wants to pray the *exact* same prayer each night, and I'm talking word for word. You'd better not leave out one name, replace one word, or get crazy and insert something new.

Then after our prayers we have hugs and high fives and kisses. Then we tuck them in, tell them we love them, and turn out their lights—making sure the nightlight is on, of course. What always felt natural and casual to my husband and me apparently has more formal components than a royal wedding!

If we leave anything out, Micah will immediately stop us and correct us. He is such a creature of habit, and lately we've been trying to teach him to be flexible and relaxed even when life doesn't go as expected. We've told him there are times when others will be praying for him if Mom and Dad are away.

While accepting different and unexpected elements overwhelms him at times, we've learned that he is, in fact, able to have a successful prayer time even without us, and even when the words are different. Micah is learning at a young age that in order to have success in life you have to bend at times, to remain calm, and overall to have a flexible outlook. Because the one time you insist on resisting change and avoiding something new could be the moment when God was going to do something miraculous in your life.

Fear of change often keeps us stuck, but it doesn't have to. God is the same yesterday, today, and tomorrow. He has promised to be with us always and never abandon us. He can redeem any situation if we'll only open our hands to receive His gifts instead of clinging to what we've lost.

MAY I HAVE THIS DANCE?

How have you faced big changes in your life? How many times have you been in a situation when all you wanted to do was throw your hands up and quit? I would venture to say most of us have been there many times. When the heat is on, that's when we need a drink of Living Water and a seat in the shade. Because I'm convinced that what you do in the shade determines how you emerge from the heat: a finisher, winner, and accomplisher—or a quitter, downer, and loser.

You see, character is created in the dark. That's right! When no one else is looking, when there are no friends or family, when no one is watching to see what you will do and how you will do it. The most wonderful professional athletes I've met are not always the ones who broke records and won championships. They are the ones who were genuinely authentic, caring, compassionate, kind men and women—not arrogant, not entitled, not prideful and full of themselves. They know their character is shaped when there are no fans around to see what they're doing. When there are no coaches, no refs, no teammates or reporters, no one looking over their shoulders.

When I was in my season of unemployment, my relationship with the Lord blossomed because I finally recognized the opportunity I had for a richer, deeper relationship with Him. What He taught me in this wilderness transformed who I am today. He did it all in a loving, inviting way. There was nothing harsh or punitive about it; He would simply remind me that He was there. For instance, on my way home from my temp job on any given night, God would whisper to me, *Can we dance when we get home?*

I would respond, "Yes, Father!" and then sometimes I would ask Him to pick the song, meaning when I turned the radio on, it would be a song He picked. Every time we danced, I was left in tears because it would always be a song dear to my heart. Then I would hold my hands up and dance around the room as if I had a physical partner. If anyone saw me, they would've thought I had absolutely *lost* it! But in my mourning, I experienced real joy as God transformed what was in my heart into dancing, both literally and figuratively.

When you're feeling stuck in life, you have to know what the Lord has called you to do, you have to see yourself there, and you have to be resilient in the midst of unexpected change and overwhelming pressure. When something you don't understand occurs and blocks your path, you must stop and ask, "Where is this taking me? How can God use this to shape my character and draw me closer to Him? What can I learn in this uncomfortable place? If I stop complaining about being stuck, what can I learn from this bend in the road?"

Yes, life will not always be comfortable as you are finding your way from the dream to the fulfillment of it. But God promises that if you pray and ask for help, He will do just that. He will be there for you. His Word tells us, "You know that under pressure, your faith-life is forced into the open and shows its true colors. So don't try to get out of anything prematurely. Let it do its work so you become mature and well-developed, not deficient in any way. If you don't know what you're doing, pray to the Father. He loves to help" (James 1:3–5 THE MESSAGE).

He will dance with you and restore your joy—true joy, not the superficial, temporary happiness you may have lost. This was so clear to me when I remained unemployed for so long. God's promises are always true, whether everything is going well or you hit a roadblock and feel stuck. He can take *any* situation and make something beautiful come out of it. He's the God of the miraculous. Remember, all He had to do was say, "Let there be light!" and there was light.

When we feel stuck, God wants us to remain teachable, flexible, and reliant on Him. It's one foot in front of the next, slowly, just baby steps, on the journey from where we are to where He wants to lead us. It's all about balance and confidence. With every step you get a bit more confident, realizing that you actually can do this.

In Stormie Omartian's book *Just Enough Light for the Step I'm On*, she said something that continues to add a little pep in the ever-challenging steps I take toward my dreams: "Each time something is required of me that I'm certain I am unable to accomplish in my own strength, I see a picture of just one or two steps being illuminated, while those before and after are engulfed in darkness and cannot be seen. This describes my walk with God."*

---

* Stormie Omartian, *Just Enough Light for the Step I'm On* (Eugene, OR: Harvest House, 2008), 7.

So when you feel trapped in a rut, when life throws an obstacle in front of you, when you feel cornered against the wall, it's time to call out to God and trust Him to lead you forward. Just pick up your foot when you feel challenged and embrace that challenge, learn from it, and keep on trucking toward your dream. Even if you're making a million photocopies, trust that you are in the right place at the right time for everything He has for you.

My personal result when I chose to be like clay and be molded revealed how I was closer to the dream God had placed inside me. He first had to do some ego demolition before He could do some character construction! What would you do if you were absolutely confident God, who's in a class all by Himself, was with you?

Think about it. How would you respond in your current circumstances if you were confident that God has a perfect plan for you and your life? Knowing and understanding the character of God will allow you to rely on Him. You will gain a better understanding that it's not by might or by power, but it's by God's Spirit that we will be successful in this life (Zech. 4:6).

If you're feeling stuck, ask your Father to help you know the next step to take and to give you the power to take it. Trust that where you are is not where you will be forever. Look ahead at what God has for you and where He wants to take you. Embrace the adventure of your present challenges and learn all He wants to teach you. Live your life to the fullest, knowing with confidence that no matter your circumstances, God is on your side!

SHIFTING RED MOMENTS
TO GREEN TRIUMPHS

GO DEEPER

When have you felt stuck in your life? How did you handle the challenges that came with this season of your life? Did you grow closer to God during this difficult time? Why or why not? What have you learned about yourself since then? About God? What's one speed bump or obstacle in your life right now that you need to bring before the Lord?

GO FURTHER

Following the prayer below or in your own words, pray for patience in your season of waiting:

Father,

Thank You for promising to be with me no matter what happens or where my path takes me. Sometimes I feel paralyzed by fear and uncertainty, longing for the safety of the past and terrified by the unknowns of the future. Help me trust You in those moments when I feel stuck and don't know what to do.

Give me the patience to wait on Your timing, the strength to endure new changes, and the courage to move forward upon Your signal. I know You are all-powerful and that nothing can stop You, Lord.

No matter what might be blocking my road right now, I'm confident You will make a path for me. I give You all the glory, honor, and praise. I love You so much!

And I pray this in Jesus' name, amen.

CHAPTER 6

MORE THAN ENOUGH

REDEFINING RED WHEN YOU'RE WEAK

Champions aren't made in the ring—
they are merely recognized there.

—JOE FRAZIER

H alle! Over here! Halle, Halle, Halle!"
Hundreds of cameras flashed at once, twinkling in quick succession like fragments of a fallen star. But the only grounded star in my line of vision was the woman coming down the red carpet toward me, the gorgeous Academy Award–winning actress Halle Berry. I was on assignment covering an awards ceremony in Los Angeles, waiting excitedly with

hundreds of fans to glimpse their favorite celebrities. With so many celebrities arriving, limos coming and going, my attention was constantly distracted—that is, until Halle arrived.

Now, I have to say, I was privileged to meet many amazing people and famous celebrities while working in television as a broadcast journalist. With the exception of meeting icons like Walter Cronkite, I usually managed to do my job and not show the excitement I felt inside while meeting these superstars.

It just came with the territory. But there were exceptions.

STARSTRUCK

When I worked for FOX Sports, our offices were on the same lot where many TV shows were filmed. Stepping outside my door to grab a cup of coffee, I passed the sets of *Ally McBeal*, *Chicago Hope*, and *NYPD Blue*. Once I began reporting for *Entertainment Tonight*, I moved to the Paramount lot where many other shows and films were shot. In fact, one of the movies made there while I was around turned out to be one of the most expensive flops in film history, *Waterworld* with Kevin Costner. The faux-ocean set was created in one of the largest parking lots on campus, which meant my colleagues and I had to park miles away as we joked about swimming to work.

Yes, I learned pretty quickly not to react when I crossed paths with Calista Flockhart, Henry Simmons, or Dennis Franz. When doing my job, I also realized that an interview with a famous person, whether an athlete or entertainer, would not go well if I was tongue-tied from being starstruck in their presence. Nonetheless, it was a thrill to meet such talented individuals on a regular basis—including sports legends like Tiger Woods, Steve McNair, and Brett Favre. (I'll never forget meeting Mr. Favre at a charity golf tournament, where he charmed me with his Southern accent and convinced me to drive his golf cart. Fortunately, we didn't crash!)

But there was something special about meeting Halle Berry that evening on the red carpet. At first glance I was surprised to see how small she was, like a fairy princess or some magical pixie from a Disney movie. While I was used to actors being much shorter and smaller in person than they looked on TV or the big screen, Ms. Berry was truly petite. The only one who remained just as big or bigger in person was Shaq!

As Halle came within a few feet of me, I smiled and greeted her. She shook my hand, and honestly, I can't remember what she said or if I even asked her the question I had prepared about that night's events. All I could do was marvel at her flawlessly smooth skin. Her skin was the color of burnished copper in her sleeveless metallic gown. She wore her famous short hairstyle, and her smile brightened the area more than any of the studio lights above us. All eyes were on her and she commanded the space with the grace and elegance of royalty.

Yes, I admit it—I was a total fan girl!

OUT OF THE DARKNESS

I'm not sure why I was so starstruck in the presence of Halle Berry—other than the obvious reasons that she's incredibly beautiful and enormously talented. I suppose I've always admired the natural, confident way she carries herself and the accessible yet classy personality she projects. Yes, I know there's often a great difference between who we perceive someone to be and who that person really is. But Halle has always impressed me as the real deal.

And I have to believe that our true character is shaped by the decisions we make and the habits we practice, particularly when we're out of the public eye—which I realize isn't very often anymore thanks to social media. But God sees our hearts all the time, even when no one else is listening or watching. Jesus told us, "There is nothing concealed that will not be disclosed, or hidden that will not be made known. What you have said in the dark will be heard in the daylight, and what you have whispered in the ear in the inner rooms will be proclaimed from the roofs" (Luke 12:2–3).

I'm convinced our character is created in the dark, those moments when only God and our conscience knows what we're doing and saying. I think of this process like a seed planted in the ground. At first that seed is in a dark place, and there in the quiet darkness a process begins. No one can see it, but the seed begins to spring forth with life beneath the cold, dark ground.

Even as the seed grows toward the light above the surface of the earth, its roots push downward, forever unseen. But these roots will propel this seed into the fullness of what it is destined to be. They will determine the kind of nutrients and the amount of water the seed receives; the roots will determine the overall health of what the seed grows and becomes.

No one even sees the roots of a plant or flower. In fact, we rarely think about them. For instance, recall the last time you admired a gorgeous flower, tree, or bush. I can virtually guarantee that you didn't think, *Wow, there must be some magnificent roots underneath this thing helping to make it look this way!* Most things out of sight remain out of mind, and so our attention is focused on the lovely red petals of the rose on a bush or the deep jade green of the ivy trailing outside our window.

Even if the roots were exposed, we would probably think them ugly in comparison to the rest of the plant they support. Nevertheless, it's those ugly roots burrowing down into a dark, dirty place that provide sustenance for the amazing plant above. Roots determine whether something will bloom and produce fruit.

Our character develops in similar fashion. At times life can feel dirty, murky, dark, and low. But it's often during those underground moments when the miraculous growth of our character takes place. Something beautiful comes out of those dark holes. Those damp, undesirable places become the wombs of something glorious.

When a woman is pregnant, her baby forms and develops inside her. All the baby's vital organs, major life functions, and even DNA are shaped and created in the mother's womb. Other than the momma growing larger physically, there is no visible evidence of the child growing and developing inside her. It's only after the baby is born that we can see the product of the process taking place inside the mother's body.

Similarly, our character is forged by the daily choices we make and the habits we cultivate, often the aspects of our lives that no one sees or pays much attention to. We wake up, get our families going, rush to work, push through another day, come home, go to bed, and then repeat the same drill the next day and the next. We may not feel like the little decisions we make matter much, at least not in the grand scheme of things.

But they do. They mean everything. Because they reveal where our time, attention, energy, and resources are invested.

They determine the roots of our character and whether it will flourish or wither with the passing of time.

PRACTICE IS NEVER OVER

Whenever I think about the way our character develops, I recall covering a Los Angeles Lakers practice one day in the late '90s. Phil Jackson was coaching a dream team that included Shaquille O'Neal, Robert Horry, Elden Campbell, Rick Fox, Eddie Jones, and Derek Fisher. Practice was pretty uneventful. Once they wrapped up, I waited to interview Eddie Jones. He was slow coming out of the locker room after practice that afternoon, and time dragged.

As I waited, I heard a number of players discussing post-workout plans. Apparently, most of them were meeting to hang out before hitting the town together. The group talking about what they were going to do that night was clearly comprised of the more veteran, cool guys on the team.

Then, after about twenty minutes, my cameraman and I watched as the janitor came in to sweep the gymnasium floor, back and forth, up and down the court. Then another gentleman came in to close off certain sections of the gym. Because their practice facility had three full-size basketball courts, they often used partitions when running a full practice. He drew two doors nearly shut, dimmed the lights, and left.

By this time, a good half hour had passed when we suddenly heard a basketball bouncing in the opposite end of the now dimly lit facility. Like watching silhouettes at dusk, we could see movement but could not discern the features of who was playing. We only heard the regular rhythm of the ball as it bounced against the backboard or swooshed through the net.

After we listened for several minutes, my photographer and I began to wonder who was over there. We joked that perhaps one of the janitors was living out his lifelong dream of being a Laker by shooting some hoops in their practice facility. Finally, Eddie Jones came out for his interview, and we temporarily forgot about our mystery dribbler. A half hour later, with my conversation with Jones taped for broadcast, my colleague and I began to pack up our equipment. Just as we were about to leave, we realized someone was *still* shooting baskets at the other end of this cavernous facility. We looked at each other and nodded, both thinking there was no way we could leave without finding out who was down there practicing for so long. It was well over an hour since practice had wrapped up, and we were the last ones there—except for whoever was still down there.

As we walked to the opposite end of this tri-court gymnasium, we chuckled again in anticipation of finding some older gentleman fulfilling his fantasy or maybe some teenager who had managed to sneak in the facility. All our silliness came to a halt as we reached the end of the dimly lit facility. To our amazement and admiration, there at the far end of the court, we saw the promising new rookie recently signed by the team: a young man named Kobe Bryant.

The youngest and therefore least-experienced player on the team, he had been signed straight out of high school, which in hoops was still unheard of back in those days. So, yes, he definitely needed to prove himself and had his work cut out for him. But there he was—doing the work. While everyone else had left to go hang, grab dinner, and have some fun, the nonconforming newbie was willing to practice and practice and practice. He was the one doing what no one else that night was willing to do.

Kobe must have felt us watching, because he turned around and looked at us curiously, perhaps wondering the same thing we'd wondered about him—why we were still there.

I simply smiled and said, "Practice is over, Kobe."

"It's never over," he replied with a chuckle.

I nodded just as the ball left his fingertips and—*whoosh*—found only net.

I have never forgotten that moment and the huge impact it had on my career. Kobe's work ethic provided him with an impressive twenty-year career, all with the Lakers, including five NBA championships. Kobe was the highest scoring player in the entire NBA for two seasons, and also scored a whopping 81 points in one game against the Toronto Raptors in January 2006.

While almost all his teammates later left for other teams, he remained a franchise superstar with the Lakers until he retired at the end of the 2015–2016 season. By that time, he had nothing left to prove to anyone. He had joined the elite of the elite, an iconic athlete known all over the world, just like Shaq or LeBron, by only his first name. For Kobe, practice was indeed never over!

He knew that passion will take you where nothing else can for the person willing to do what no one else is willing to do.

PERFECT IN WEAKNESS

Kobe's example is extraordinary proof that what we do in the dark determines *how* we do in the light. For us as Christians, if we choose to follow God, to obey His commandments, and to abide by His standards, our character develops in a healthy, vibrant way that leads to maturity as we become all our Father created us to be. If we're willing to go the extra mile and give all we have for the kingdom, we become the best we can be. What we practice leads to how we play the game.

The psalmist expressed this perfectly in his very first song: "Blessed is the one who does not walk in step with the wicked or stand in the way that sinners take or sit in the company of mockers, but whose delight is in the law of the LORD, and who meditates on his law day and night. That person is like a tree planted by streams of water, which yields its fruit in season and whose leaf does not wither—whatever they do prospers" (Ps. 1:1–3).

Our choices in the dark moments of life matter. When we're hurting, disappointed, and struggling, we may be tempted to go our own way instead of God's. Some people try to take control and create an idol that provides them with what they crave and think they need most—money, sex, fame, career, family, even church. Others feel overwhelmed by life's demands and escape into addictions that temporarily provide hits of pleasure to dull their senses and alleviate their pain.

Instead of trying to look elsewhere for help or relief, we must remember to trust God no matter what we're going through. Even in the midst of our weakest moments—or more accurately, especially in the midst of our weakest moments—we can rely on our Father's strength to see us through. In fact, our need for God is actually a gift because we're forced to depend on Him rather than becoming convinced we can take care of life's problems by ourselves. Paul shared how he struggled with a "thorn in the flesh" that he asked God to remove. But the answer he received is one we must remember as well:

Even if I should choose to boast, I would not be a fool, because I would be speaking the truth. But I refrain, so no one will think more of me than is warranted by what I do or say, or because of these surpassingly great revelations. Therefore, in order to keep me from becoming conceited, I was given a thorn in my flesh, a messenger of Satan, to torment me. Three times I pleaded with the Lord to take it away from me. But he said to me, "My grace is sufficient for you, for my power is made perfect in weakness." Therefore I will boast all the more gladly about my weaknesses, so that Christ's power may rest on me. That is why, for Christ's sake, I delight in weaknesses, in insults, in hardships, in persecutions, in difficulties. For when I am weak, then I am strong. (2 Cor. 12:6–10)

You might recall that Paul had once been known as Saul before he had a dramatic encounter with Christ while traveling on the road to Damascus. Saul had kept a perfect track record within the Jewish religious traditions to which his family adhered. They believed a person's righteousness could only be achieved by strictly following God's Law. Consequently, Saul thought he was above everyone else because of how hard he worked to follow all the commandments and obey all the rules.

No wonder he felt totally justified in his persecution of people going around talking about grace and forgiveness in the name of Jesus Christ, whom Saul likely considered a criminal heretic. But after he met Jesus, Saul started going by the Roman version of his name, Paul, and spreading the good news of the gospel beyond Israel and to all the Gentiles in foreign lands.

Paul often wrote letters to the communities of believers in these distant locations, and many of these divinely inspired messages became part of what we call the New Testament. This explains why Paul wrote to the church at Corinth, encouraging them not to forfeit their faith or give up on what they believed. To keep it real, Paul made sure these other believers knew that he was far from perfect and had struggles in his life just as they did. We don't know specifically what he struggled with, but Paul described it as a "thorn in my flesh" and a "messenger of Satan" (v. 7). That sounds painful enough for me!

Even more insightful than merely sharing that he had this struggle, Paul knew God allowed him to keep struggling with this issue for a reason, namely so Paul would remain humble and dependent on the Lord (v. 7). But just like you and I have done with issues in our own lives, Paul prayed for God to deliver him from this problem three times. But God's answer was the same each time: "My grace is sufficient for you, for my power is made perfect in weakness" (v. 9).

Rather than being disappointed like we might be, Paul *rejoiced* in God's reply because he knew it meant he would be forced to continue relying on God.

Paul couldn't remove this problem or alleviate its pain, and God wouldn't remove it for him. Paul had to live with it and face it daily, persevering in the midst of all the other circumstances of his life. But what he discovered remains just as relevant for us today: "When I am weak, then I am strong" (v. 10).

EXPECT GOD'S POWER

I'm convinced this is the secret to true growth in character and maturity in our faith. We have to take the focus off our weakness and what we lack and focus instead on God's strength and divine power. So often in our journeys of faith, we have to do what we can't imagine doing and keep going when we feel we have nothing left to give. But the only way to do this is through the power of God's Spirit dwelling in us.

With God's help, you can go beyond your limits and accomplish so much more than what you can do when you settle for your own abilities or someone else's. In fact, one of my favorite mottos reminds us that "the status quo is not enough." In other words, what everyone else is doing isn't enough to sustain us through life's storms and strengthen our characters in the midst of crises. If you live by a popular standard, then you will only be as good as everyone else.

So what will separate you from the rest? What will put you on another platform? What will elevate you? As I've learned, you have to be willing to go where no one else wants to go. You have to be the first one at the office and the last one to go home. You have to study at home when you're off. You have to do whatever it takes to be the best. You have to work when everyone else is shopping at the mall. You have to have a passion that causes you to keep going when all you want to do is quit. You have to channel your inner Kobe and keep practicing! Like Paul, you must allow God's power to shine through the areas of weakness in your life.

Yes, you will have good and bad days; such is life. But what you do with both types of days is critical. We all know success most of the time doesn't happen overnight. We all wish it did. But most of the time, we have to work at it for a while and be patient as we are perfecting our skill. Often patience is required, along with practice and perseverance. Many times when we have struggled for a long time, we are closer to God than we would be otherwise. And as we grow closer to Him, we discover that He's been making a miracle out of our mess all along.

I'm reminded of a woman whose story is in the Bible. She suffered from chronic internal bleeding, perhaps from a tumor or other disease. During New Testament times it was common practice in difficult medical cases for people to consult many different doctors and receive a variety of treatments. Luke, a physician as well as the author of the gospel of Luke, suggested that the woman was not helped because her condition was incurable: "Now a woman, having a flow of blood for twelve years . . . spent all her livelihood on physicians and could not be healed by any" (Luke 8:43 NKJV).

Word got to her that Jesus was in town. Having heard of His healing power, she had faith that if she could get to Him, she could be healed. I like the way the book of Mark tells the story from this point:

> When she heard about Jesus, she came behind Him in the crowd and touched His garment. For she said, "If only I may touch His clothes, I shall be made well."
>
> Immediately the fountain of her blood was dried up, and she felt in her body that she was healed of the affliction. . . .
>
> And He said to her, "Daughter, your faith has made you well. Go in peace, and be healed of your affliction." (Mark 5:27–29, 34 NKJV)

This woman expected that her situation was about to change. She anticipated being healed and believed that Jesus was a healer.

Something happens when we have expectancy, when we expect a situation to change, when we expect our circumstances to shift, when we invite God into our weakness.

On the other side of your expectancy often lies your miracle!

For in that moment, Jesus said to her, "Your faith has made you well." In other words, her faith and its inherent hopeful expectancy played an important role in her healing and fulfillment.

Are you willing to invite God into the weak cracks in the foundation of your soul? Will you trust Him and keep trusting Him for a miracle, even if, like Paul, it doesn't turn out quite the way you want? Where is your expectation today? This woman's story is a perfect example of where real, heartfelt expectation will take you. Open-hearted faith is a simple, yet critical, component to the growth and healthy development of our character.

Who you are has everything to do with what you are doing, and what you are doing has everything to do with where you are going. You may not be a movie star like Halle Berry or a superstar athlete like Kobe Bryant, but if you're just an ordinary person like Elictia Hart, committed to an extraordinary God, then you can trust Him with your weakness. We may be faced with situations that make us see red, with thorns in our lives that cut us so we definitely see red, but in those moments, remember that red means go to your ultimate power source.

SHIFTING RED MOMENTS
TO GREEN TRIUMPHS

GO DEEPER

Who are your personal heroes and role models who have influenced the way your character has developed? What traits within yourself have you strengthened by following their examples? What areas of weakness are you presently aware need strengthening in your life? How have you experienced God's power in these areas? What are you still waiting and hoping for Him to do in these weak places?

GO FURTHER

Lord,

Too often I use my weaknesses as an excuse for giving in to temptation or turning from You and taking matters into my own hands. Forgive me, Father, for those moments when I have depended on anything or anyone other than You.

Thank You for giving me Your power to get through the storms of life and to accomplish what I could never do on my own. Give me strength to focus on the daily habits and small decisions that can have consequences for Your kingdom.

Let who I am in the dark corners of life glorify You just as much as when I'm in the spotlight. I love You, God, and want You to be the source for everything I am and everything I do.

Amen.

CHAPTER 7

TIME WILL TELL

REDEFINING RED WHEN YOU'RE WAITING

The principle part of faith is patience.
—George MacDonald

Despite my success as a broadcast journalist, I began to long for more than the adrenaline rush of the next big story in a fast-paced twenty-four-hour news cycle. I wanted a husband and children and a permanent place where we could create our home. I knew I could have both, my career and a family, but more and more I felt pulled in a new direction, one that led to new relationships in a permanent community. But there was something else. I couldn't put my finger on it at the time, but soon enough I would realize ministry was part of God's plan for my life.

Flash forward ten years and instead of standing in front of a camera talking about the Lakers or greeting Halle Berry, I found myself preaching the gospel in front of thousands of people. In the remaining chapters I'll tell you more about how I wound up there alongside my husband, a pastor. But for now, I'll just say that transitioning from my career to family and full-time ministry required me to change the way I viewed time. You see, I had always known that our timing is not necessarily God's timing, but a visit overseas recently reminded me that God is always on the move even when we feel stuck.

I had been invited to speak at a ministry conference in Burkina Faso, a beautiful landlocked country in West Africa. Formerly a French colony and called the Republic of Upper Volta for several decades as it pursued independence, Burkina Faso is home to more than seventeen million native residents. Humbled and thrilled to accept the invitation, I began preparing and looking forward to the trip. As part of my preparation, a team of prayer warriors from our church committed to praying for me and for all that God wanted to do there.

From these prayer sessions, one dear sister, a wise mother of our church, called to tell me that while praying God revealed to her that on my trip I would face a power surge. She was confident in this message, although she wasn't sure whether this meant a literal surge like you see with electrical power when it trips a breaker in your home or a spiritual power surge from the strength of the Holy Spirit.

As I soon found out, it was both!

Before I could even leave the United States, I was reminded of this dear sister's prophetic message. Flying from Omaha to Burkina Faso required changing planes in Minneapolis, and as the team from our church raced to our gate, suddenly everything around us in this fifteen-foot radius went dark. If you've ever been in a public place, such as a store or business, when the power goes off, you know how strange and surreal it can feel. One minute you're deciding which brand of ketchup to buy, and the next you can't see your shopping cart! Only in my case, we were able to see at least a little because everything around us was still lit up. It was just a small circle around us that had lost power. Crazy, right?

I looked at my friend Miriam. We thought, *This is unusual*, but we kept walking. The curious feeling lingered. What exactly was God up to? What did this mean?

We continued on our journey and arrived at the capital city's airport without further incident. Unless you count the amazingly warm and beautiful welcoming committee who was there to greet us upon arriving! Our small team had expected that one or two people would pick us up and take us to our hotel, but instead we were greeted by dozens of people—singers and dancers and children with bouquets of flowers for us! It was lovely, and despite being awake for almost thirty-six hours, our team did our best to show our appreciation.

After catching up on some of our sleep, it was time to head to the venue where the conference would be held, a stadium that probably held about seventy thousand people. While I had wondered how many people would actually show up, I wasn't prepared for the overflow crowd that assembled for the opening session and every session that followed. Despite the sweltering heat and humidity and the dust that seemed to constantly sift through the air, thousands of men, women, and children had come from every direction. They walked, rode bikes, piled into the backs of flatbed trucks, shared scooters, crammed into cars, and rode donkeys and horses. People sat in the packed-dirt aisles while others clustered near the entrances to hear the message of God's Word being preached.

After an uplifting time of worship and praise, the invited speakers began to teach and preach. I was nervous, of course, but trusted that God had me there for a reason. I prayed that His Spirit would simply speak through me. When it was my turn to preach, I went to the stage, waved to the audience, and took the microphone in hand. In that moment, all the electricity went out! The lights dimmed and the sound system stopped working. The crowd immediately buzzed with curiosity and slight alarm, wondering what had happened.

I knew immediately what had happened! And as I looked at Miriam standing at the side of the stage, it was at this moment we thought about what our dear sister had said; this was a power surge. The lights may have been off, but God's power was definitely on! After it became apparent that the power was not going to come right back on, various members of the conference team and host church began strolling down the aisles, stopping to pray and preach with various seated sections. It felt like revival was breaking out! No electricity was needed for the power of the gospel to charge the people in that place with hope.

Finally, about twenty-five minutes later, the power returned and I took the stage once again and preached like never before. God moved through me like an electrical current and lovingly shocked the audience there with the immense power of His love and grace. Many people came to know the Lord that evening, and I would venture that every soul there was blessed. I know I sure was!

If that experience had ended right there, I would have been more than happy and impressed by God's power and the gift of the prophetic word about that power surge. But do you know what? The next day, when it was my turn to take the stage—again, after several other guests had taught and preached—I took the microphone in hand, and it happened again. The lights flickered and the power faded. Please believe me, because I can't make this stuff up!

The blackout lasted only about fifteen minutes this second time, and we wasted no time waiting on it to return. Along with dozens of others, I immediately went into the aisle and began to preach, trusting that the people God wanted to hear my voice would hear me just fine without a microphone or any amplification. The Spirit of God was upon us all that day, and once again, we knew we didn't need electricity to experience a surge of power unlike any other!

WHAT ARE YOU WAITING ON?

I share this experience with you because I suspect we sometimes feel like we can't proceed spiritually until our expectations are met. We might think God can't use us to reach others until we've become more spiritually mature or feel confident in our faith. We may even feel stuck in a season, waiting on God to do something we think has to happen before we can move forward and continue living out the purpose for which He designed us. But I'm not sure that's true.

My experiences related to this trip in Burkina Faso remind me that we often hit pause when God wants us to keep going. We feel impatient and assume we must wait until the power comes on again, but God wants us to trust Him as we step out in the dark. We feel like we're caught in transition, but if we trust the Holy Spirit, we can minister each and every day, no matter the circumstances surrounding us.

I wonder if part of our impatience is the result of our fast-paced, get-it-now culture. Do you remember the impact of the microwave? Who would have thought you could have a steaming hot bag of buttery popcorn in only two minutes? At my house you needed a pan with a lid, a little bit of cooking oil, some popcorn kernels, and some elbow grease to shake it around for nine or ten minutes until those kernels started dancing. But once the microwave became popularly accepted, foods made especially for microwave cooking soon followed.

These days our world changes at dizzying speed, and we become conditioned to lose patience if we can't have our popcorn, our downloadable file, or our favorite movie in a matter of seconds. Our spiritual lives, however, continue to run on God's timing, in which it usually takes longer for change to occur than a couple of minutes. And at the same time, it doesn't require us to wait to begin serving and ministering to others. In Burkina Faso, we could have waited until the power was restored in the stadium before starting to minister. But the Holy Spirit doesn't require electricity, so there was no need to wait! I'm convinced God prepared me for His power surges in order to help me change the way I think about His timing.

You may be experiencing the same kind of spiritual power surge yourself. Maybe you've been praying for God to change you in some specific way for a long time—months, years, or even decades. But as much as you want to change, as much as you've prayed for God to change you and to transform your circumstances, nothing seems to happen. In the meantime, you just keep running in place, afraid to step out and take the opportunities that God sets before you.

But you don't have to wait! Just because you're still waiting on God to complete His work in you doesn't mean God isn't already at work. What if this waiting period is simply your own power surge? It appears that you're stuck in the dark, but really God is equipping you to handle the enormous burst of power you're about to receive!

You may be on the cusp of incredible change in your life, a realization of the amazing potential that you've been waiting on for a long time. Events in your life right now may propel you into something new and purposeful, something God is doing in your life if you will let Him. God's Word tells us, "'I know the plans I have for you,' declares the LORD, 'plans to prosper you and not to harm you, plans to give you hope and a future'" (Jer. 29:11). The Lord may want to zap you with a miracle faster than a microwave makes popcorn, or He may want to transform you more slowly. Either way, you remain connected to your ultimate power source—the Holy Spirit.

TIME FOR CHANGE

Sometimes we want our lives to change, but we're standing in our own way. We think we must wait on God when He's waiting on us! We're so busy clinging to old expectations that God can't give us what we've asked Him for, let alone something better. If you're feeling stuck in your current season of life, if you've grown so impatient that you're tempted to give up on God's timing, I encourage you to redefine this red moment as an indicator that you need to make some changes in order to make room for God to work.

Perhaps the place to start looking for the change you desire in your life is to examine the various ways you spend your time. Being cognizant of what you are spending your time doing will not only help you be more productive, but it will also reveal where your energy is being invested. Typically whatever is important to you is what you will devote your time to doing.

If God is truly a priority in your life, you will spend time reading the Bible, living according to what the Bible suggests, and growing in community at church or somewhere with other believers. If family is important, you will naturally spend time with your spouse, children, and other family members. If you value being physically fit and as healthy as possible, then you will spend time working out. Again, you will make time for the relationships, activities, and life goals that are the most valuable to you.

You may know what you want your priorities to be, but are those areas where you are investing your time, energy, and resources? It's one thing to say you put God first, but if the only time you're in His Word is in the sermon on Sunday mornings, then you have a problem: what you say matters most is not what you are most devoted to cultivating. If you say your family comes first, but you consistently work weekends and miss special moments—birthdays, ballgames, recitals—your actions are not backing up your words.

From time to time, I like to do an internal audit of my calendar and see exactly where the past week ended up being spent. How much time did I spend each day in prayer? In reading and meditating on the Bible? In loving and serving my husband and children? In helping friends, neighbors, and others in my community? Sometimes it's shocking how little time actually went where I wanted it to go.

Sure, we all have seasons when our schedules are disrupted by an unexpected tragedy, family problem, or career disruption. But most of the time, you should have a keen awareness of whether your time each day goes where you want it to go. If you don't know what's important to you, think back over the last couple of weeks and see where you spent the bulk of your free time. This will help pinpoint what you value.

I encourage you to conduct your own time audit right now, pausing to look over your calendar on your phone or tablet or however you keep track of your daily and weekly schedule. Does the way you've been spending your time reflect what you care about most? Or do you need to make some adjustments? Are you waiting on something that you don't need before you move forward?

PASSING LIKE A SHADOW

Time is our most valuable asset, and once it is gone, we can never get it back. Money comes and goes, possessions wear out or get stolen, and even family heirlooms can be replaced. But your time here on earth is limited—you have a finite amount of days left to live. The psalms frequently and poetically remind us of this truth: "Man is like a breath; his days are like a passing shadow" (Ps. 144:4 ESV) and, "My days are like an evening shadow; I wither away like grass" (Ps. 102:11 ESV). While we usually don't like to consider our mortality, it doesn't change the reality that our physical bodies are passing away.

All the more reason to focus on what is eternal. Having an eternal perspective on our choices, relationships, and investments can help us make sure our actions align with our priorities. Because everything we do requires some level of an investment of time. Time is the vehicle that will get you from one place to the next. Time is the vehicle that God uses to move us along in this life.

Throughout the Bible, God maneuvers within the confines of time. Although He created time, God is not subject to it. He is bigger than time and is not limited by its linear, progressive limitations.

While we live in a physical world with its four known space-time dimensions of length, width, height (or depth), and time, God dwells in a different dimension—the spiritual realm—beyond the perception of our physical senses. The Bible tells us God is Spirit (John 4:24). And it's not that God isn't real; it's a matter of His not being limited by the physical laws and dimensions that govern our world (Isa. 57:15). He created these laws, but He's not subject to them.

The psalmist used a simple yet profound analogy in describing the timelessness of God: "A thousand years in your sight are like a day that has just gone by, or like a watch in the night" (Ps. 90:4). The eternity of God is contrasted with the temporality of human beings. Our lives are but short and frail, but God does not weaken or fail with the passage of time. His omnipotence and omniscience exist beyond the boundaries of the temporal world we live in.

Amazingly, although the Lord doesn't have to, He often chooses to "crawl" into our mortal limitations of space and time in order to take us from where we are to where we are going. He also gives us some points of reference about time in the book of Ecclesiastes, emphasizing that there's a time and a season for everything under the sun. In other words, there's a time to remain where you are in terms of your dreams, and there's a time for advancement. The big thing is being aware of how you spend your time as you try to discern the current season you are in.

WHAT TIME IS IT?

How can you be aware of your current season of life, and how you should spend your time? How can you practice patience and trust God's timing and not your own urgency? I've found two factors that often help reveal what season you are in, which in turn provides direction for how best to invest your time. These guidelines involve your sight (mental and spiritual) and your chronological age.

Knowing where you are (*sight*) on your journey and when it's time (*age*) to move on or press toward your next goal will keep you in the season God intends for you to be in. While our chronological seasons of life do not always align with our spiritual seasons, we still need to be aware that the two are closely related. If we're not walking with the Lord, then we may lose sight of His direction and the season to which He's calling us—all the more reason to trust God each step of the way. His Word tells us, "To everything there is a season, a time for every purpose under heaven" (Eccl. 3:1 NKJV).

Setting your schedule to reflect the future to which God calls you requires insight into your unique purpose in life. Knowing who God created you to be and the very special and unique purpose for which He designed you can help you make other important decisions. Seeing yourself living out the dream He has placed in your heart casts a vision forward into your future. With this current goal as your divine destination, you can work backward and ask yourself, "How can I spend my time today so that I step closer to that place I know God wants me to be?"

In my own life, I could see myself stair-stepping through the journalism ladder. This was the *sight* aspect of what I felt called to do, and therefore determined how I should spend my time. As a result, I worked as hard as possible to be the best me in that role I could be. I began behind the scenes. And with every position, I could visually see myself doing the next job as I worked to do my best at fulfilling my current role.

Because I was single with no children all those years, I was afforded the opportunity to spend my time working hard, doing what many were not able or willing to do in order to gain valuable wisdom and knowledge about my position, which then propelled me forward into the next season and its new responsibilities and challenges. This was my *age* aspect.

As a career-focused woman, I often heard it said that there would be time later to marry and start a family. This always made sense to me because I knew the crazy demands of my job required all my time, energy, and attention. It's quite difficult to give a husband and children the time they deserve and still devote quality time to progressing up the ladder in whatever field you are in. On the other hand, I have seen other career-minded individuals marry early, have families, raise kiddos, and then press hard for advancement when their kids are a bit older.

Simply put, there is no perfect or magical formula. Whatever the Lord has for you is what's perfect. Whatever God wants done, He is able to make it happen through us if we are attentive and responsive to His guidance. Remember, only He has our blueprints. At times He will reveal more of those blueprints to us than at other times. As long as we are staying the course and looking toward our God-given goal, we should be able to clearly identify the season we're in and accordingly how we're spending our time.

Once you know who you are and what you are doing, it's hard not to have a clearer understanding of your purpose. Being able to answer these questions should also help you connect some dots. The key word in the previous sentence is *should*. The truth is, we often don't know what we are supposed to do next. Sometimes the future seems unclear as we wait on the Lord to reveal His direction for us.

You can be young, old, or somewhere in between, and it's quite possible to still be discovering your God-given dreams and what you are supposed to be doing. But here's a little secret: once you have figured out who you are and what you are doing, it's so much easier to gain understanding of where you are going. And once you know where you're going, you can set your schedule in such a way to move in that direction!

Once you know who you are in Christ and understand your purpose, you're well on your way. You can see yourself moving in a certain direction while spending your time creating momentum in the same direction. Who you are and what you are doing has everything to do with where you are going.

It's like planning a vacation. You first determine the kind of vacation you want to have—the beach or the mountains, an amusement park or a camping trip, a rural retreat or an urban adventure—which is usually based on the kind of person God made you to be. Then you have to decide where specifically you're going and when you're going to leave. Then it's time to start your travels until you're there! Unless you have a major catastrophe or God changes your previously arranged travel plans, you will end up where you were headed, enjoying your trip along the way.

And as an old saying reminds us, the joy is in the journey.

PATIENCE IN THE PROCESS

While working in the world of professional sports and entertainment, I often saw a player, actor, or singer suddenly have their big breakout moment. It might have been during a crucial game in the playoffs or in a heart-wrenching scene on the big screen. It might have been when they unexpectedly shone brighter than anyone expected in the end zone or in the spotlight. While the world hailed these new stars as "overnight sensations," I knew that it had taken them years and years to get to that moment when they got their shot.

Like Kobe Bryant practicing on that dimly lit court for hours after practice had ended for everyone else, we must recognize that practice never ends in this lifetime. At the very least, we must practice patience as we prepare for the big moments ahead. This is easier said than done. Thanks to YouTube, reality TV, and social media, many people think they should be able to rocket into fame and fortune the first time they try. But the true stars in any field know that it takes discipline, practice, and tons of passion to persevere and be their best. They have to embrace the process before they can embrace the proceeds.

And like it or not, every process takes time. Often we get

rushed to see things accomplished and attain success, but most of the time we need a bit of patience so the process can effectively play out. I love the example that Jesus provided for us with the story of Lazarus in the Bible.

> Now a man named Lazarus was sick. He was from Bethany, the village of Mary and her sister Martha. . . . So the sisters sent word to Jesus, "Lord, the one you love is sick."
>
> When he heard this, Jesus said, "This sickness will not end in death. No, it is for God's glory so that God's Son may be glorified through it." Now Jesus loved Martha and her sister and Lazarus. So when he heard that Lazarus was sick, he stayed where he was two more days, and then he said to his disciples, "Let us go back to Judea" . . .
>
> On his arrival, Jesus found that Lazarus had already been in the tomb for four days. . . .
>
> "Lord," Martha said to Jesus, "if you had been here, my brother would not have died. But I know that even now God will give you whatever you ask."
>
> Jesus said to her, "Your brother will rise again." (John 11:1, 3–7, 17, 21–23)

The role of God's perfect timing in this story cannot be underestimated. Jesus used the element of waiting to shift Martha's mind-set. Instead of immediately rushing back to see Lazarus, Jesus maintained the schedule of His Father's divine plan—for Jesus and for Lazarus as well as for Mary and Martha. He cultivated patience in His dear friends that at first glance might seem indifferent or even coldhearted. Instead, it's just the opposite! Jesus loved these friends so much that He wanted to use this opportunity to deepen their faith in Him even as He gave His Father all the glory for the miracle of raising Lazarus from the dead.

This required a paradigm shift for Martha. She already believed Jesus could heal the sick and change water into wine. But there she reached the limits of her understanding of what the Messiah could do. Her truth, like our own so much of the time, was incomplete because it was based only on past experience. She was fully aware that He was the Miracle Worker, and that's why she said, "Lord, if you had been here, my brother would not have died." But that statement in itself is only partially true, because Jesus could have kept Lazarus from dying, and He didn't even need to be there!

Christ could have spoken the word and instantly cured His friend many miles away. But I'm convinced this miracle was about more than just raising the dead. Jesus wanted to use the process of waiting, hoping, and daring to believe to shift Mary's and Martha's mind-sets. Even after Jesus told Martha her brother would rise again, she misunderstood and thought Jesus was talking about the final judgment when all shall rise (John 11:24). Her understanding of mortality and even the afterlife were limited by what she knew—and what she knew was incomplete.

By waiting until after Lazarus had been dead for four days— not one, not two, not even three, but *four* days!—Jesus made a powerful statement. Basically, He said, "I am not confined to time or place. I am not confined to what you perceive is possible. I am not confined to what you know or think you know."

He had to allow them to *wait* for Lazarus to die. As painful as it was for them, and perhaps for Jesus in knowing they were grieving, He allowed them to experience a greater miracle than just the healing of the sick. He not only fulfilled their desperate prayers, Jesus exceeded what they imagined God could do.

GIVE US PATIENCE NOW

Now, let's be honest: waiting is painful. We all hate waiting. From when we're the age of my kids—who can't get in our car without asking, "Are we there yet? How long will it take?"—until we're taking our last breaths and anticipating heaven, almost all people struggle with patience. As the old saying goes, "I want patience and I want it now!"

I seriously don't know one person who would line up to wait for a blessing. Most people would get on the "right now" bus. In our society, the social norm is to hurry up in order to enjoy immediate gratification. From fast food to speed dating to nanosecond wire transfers, we like life to move at the speed of light. The more things a company can produce, and the sooner they can produce them, the better, right? The more products someone can produce and the quicker they can produce them, the more money can be made.

While we are all rushing around trying to make things quicker so events will happen sooner, God must be chuckling to Himself. The process of spiritual transformation, in which we grow into the likeness of Christ, has no shortcuts. It takes as long as it takes. And in the meantime, we might as well make peace with practicing patience in the process.

In the Bible we're told God has made everything beautiful in its time (Eccl. 3:11). Often I suspect our heavenly Father is telling us, "Don't hurry Me. Don't worry, My child—I've got this. Just relax and keep waiting. Don't rush Me." I can't help but believe that so many of the things we're waiting on are simply a matter of deepening our faith in Him and teaching us to adjust to His eternal perspective instead of our limited, temporal point of view.

In making them wait, Jesus told Mary and Martha, "I need to shift what you perceive is true." It's basically like learning how to solve advanced math equations. We have to let go of certain limitations in order to grasp the new, bigger, and different system and its variables. Our thinking capacities are limited by being human, but we also tend to like things to make sense, to be orderly and logical, with a clear relationship among the pieces of any puzzle.

The directions and decisions to which God calls us will not always make sense from a human perspective. If you tell your friend, "I believe the Lord has called me to quit my job and start a business," and your friend can't imagine how you can go from the point of quitting your present job to achieving this new business, such a move seems crazy. For very logical reasons, that friend may not be able to see you progressing from being an employee to owning your own business.

And because they can't see that progression, they're not able to accept the idea of you not working at your job. They are not able to see you not there, because they can't forsake that thought process of how they see you and understand the situation. Mary was unable to forsake what she perceived to be the truth about her brother's death and Jesus' ability to heal him. Even though she knew and trusted Jesus as the Messiah, she didn't have the capacity yet to wait on what was coming.

God may have kept you waiting on something you wanted for a very long time. He may have ignited a dream in you that's been simmering for years, decades even, and still the flame hasn't caught and burned into a bigger blaze. The embers haven't died, but neither have they burned brighter. You can't understand why you're stuck in between, still hoping and wondering and waiting. But the time will come when God pours the fuel of opportunity over the embers of your dream so they erupt like wildfire.

TIME AND TIME AGAIN

To cultivate patience in our process, we must remember that as Christians we operate in two different systems of time. One is *chronos*, the earthly forward movement of one moment after another, and the other is *kairos*, a pattern of time that operates within God's eternal perspective according to His divine will for our lives. We experience both right now, which isn't always easy to remember, especially when we're tired of waiting. But understanding how each one operates can make it just a little bit easier.

Chronos is time as we usually think of it—the seconds, minutes, hours, days, weeks, months, and years we use to measure the passing of time in our lives. As the saying goes, this kind of time waits for no one, and all are subject to its passing. It doesn't matter who you are; it doesn't matter where you've come from; it doesn't matter how old you are or how young you are, how skinny, rich, short, or tall you are, who your mother is, or who your father is. It doesn't matter if you live in Africa or Alabama; all of us are governed and must function or live under *chronos*. No one can bend *chronos* or add an extra hour to the twenty-four assigned to comprise one day.

Kairos time, on the other hand, exists as an opportunity,

a moment outside of *chronos* time. It's a moment that literally changes everything from the moment that preceded it. It's usually unexpected, surprising, and even shocking. Some people call a *kairos* moment a coincidence, but I like to think of it as the supernatural now.

We experience *kairos* time in the moment when God steps into our situation and does something miraculous for us. It's when you had no money to pay your bills but a check comes in the mail. It's when the doctor said there is no cure for your condition and you are healed. It's when your child is out of control and lost in this world and comes home as if they had never left.

Kairos moments are God moments, miracles, divine turning points that others may have deemed impossible. It's the instant when Lazarus came back to life, when the lame man was healed, when the water became wine. The Bible tells us, "With man this is impossible, but with God all things are possible" (Matt. 19:26). That remains one of my favorite scriptures, and it always gives me hope when a situation appears hopeless. It assures us of God's presence in those *kairos* moments of life and allows us to dream when it appears our dreams are dead. It allows us to have joy when our hearts are broken. It reminds us of timeless truth, that God is forever a God of *kairos* possibilities in the face of *chronos* impossibilities.

So never underestimate the power of a moment, my friend! When you feel stuck at a crossroads in life and the red light refuses to change, just remember that red means go to God. His timing will always be better for us than what we perceive on our watches, clocks, and calendars. As the old saying goes, "God may not show up when you want Him to, but He's always on time!"

SHIFTING RED MOMENTS
TO GREEN TRIUMPHS

GO DEEPER

What are you waiting on right now in your life? How long have you been waiting? What have you heard from God regarding this longing in your heart? What has He shown you or taught you during this interval as you continue to wait? How have you grown closer to Him in the midst of your time of waiting? What could you be doing to move forward instead of simply waiting?

GO FURTHER

Lord,

It's so hard to wait sometimes, and I thank You for staying with me no matter what happens or where I find myself in life. I know You have a plan for me, a good plan that is for my best interests, so help me to wait patiently on Your timing and not give in to despair or to reckless rebellion in an attempt to take time into my own hands.

Remind me, God, that I am bound by chronos time but that You are beyond this realm of time in the supernatural realm of kairos time. Give me eyes to see the eternal, and help me look beyond the temporary comforts and conveniences I so often want.

I praise You for all You're doing in my life, Lord. For the things I can see and the things I will never see until I am with You in heaven.

I pray this all in Jesus' name, amen.

CHAPTER 8

IN THE CROSSHAIRS

REDEFINING RED WHEN YOU'RE IN DANGER

*When I dare to be powerful—to
use my strength in the service of my
vision, then it becomes less and less
important whether I am afraid.*

—AUDRE LORDE

As pastors, my husband and I often travel to preach, teach, and minister in churches around the globe. Sometimes we get to go together, but often one of us will go and the other will stay home with our kids. These mission trips are always exciting and filled with dramatic moments of seeing God at work. One trip in particular, however, a visit to beautiful Brazil, will forever stand out in my memory.

Along with my friend Jodi and my sister-in-law Teena from our home church in Omaha, I first flew into Sao Paolo, Brazil, and then again north to the coast city of Fortaleza, which I learned means "stronghold" or "fortress" in Portuguese, the native language there. From our hosts as well as others who had visited, I'd heard a lot about the beauty of Fortaleza with its sugar-sand beaches, turquoise waters, and friendly smiles from its more than three million residents.

By the time we finally arrived in Fortaleza, our team had been traveling for more than twenty-four hours and we felt like zombies—too exhausted to stand but too tired to sleep. It was still early evening after we checked in to our hotel, so we decided to stay up a few hours longer in order to adjust to the local time. We knew we didn't want to venture too far, so we decided to walk the few short blocks down to the beach.

Warm, sea-scented air greeted us as we took in the shops, buildings, and restaurants leading to the nearby seashore. Traffic sounds harmonized with blaring music and the loud chatter of tourist groups. The bustling city reminded me of Miami with the way its dynamic urban life runs right up to the natural beauty of its beaches.

Living up to its tourist-brochure description, the shoreline extended as far as I could see with nothing but blue surf kissing powdery sands. Before long we came upon rows of stalls, which the locals called a fair, where people were selling various goods they had made—baskets, hats, T-shirts, key chains, jewelry, beach souvenirs, you name it. Vendors sold tropical fruit drinks and other native delicacies. With many families strolling and browsing along the sandy aisle of this outdoor shopping mall, the fun, lively atmosphere revived us.

But not for long.

AFTER DARK

We shopped and purchased a few items as we watched the setting sun burn an orange and gold trail along the horizon over the water. We had been there a couple of hours, and it began getting dark, so we started back toward our hotel. Once evening descended, probably around 9:00 p.m., we noticed a shift in the atmosphere. Retracing the route back to our hotel, we began to notice girls on the street, some alone but mostly in small packs, young girls that could not have been older than eleven or twelve. Their skimpy outfits showed off tan bodies and faces glaring with makeup. Loitering in the shadows of alleys and storefronts, they were clearly doing their job and waiting for customers.

Now, the sight of any female selling herself on the street would have been disturbing enough, but seeing these young girls, these children, made my spirit ache and my stomach queasy. It was just so disheartening to see the way everyone around us acted like this was a totally normal scene—but there was nothing normal about it.

As we passed them huddled in small groups, we noticed many feminized boys within their midst as well, either cross-dressing or somewhere in the process of a transgender procedure. One in particular caught our attention, a tall beautifully made-up young teen holding the hand of a little girl. This attention-getter was as beautiful as any young woman you might see, but there were little signs—a prominent Adam's apple, big feet, the hint of a beard—that created enough cognitive dissonance to make us look twice.

As it happened, the two of them started walking a few steps ahead of us in the same direction, finally stopping at an open-air McDonald's along the way.

Teena, Jodi, and I were so taken with the two of them that we followed them just to get a better look and see if our eyes were playing tricks on us or not. Our brains couldn't process how this stunning young person, with the slim build and athletic stride of a boy, could have such flawless olive skin, high cheekbones, beautiful eyes, and ruby lips. And his "little sister" was just as beautiful and just as heavily made up.

We were probably gawking, but my friends and I just kept watching them, trying to read their eyes and see into their lives. Without thinking about it, we probably thought we could some-how learn something about who they were, maybe even help them in some way. But soon we realized that this wasn't like any McDonald's we had been in before. The lines were crowded with customers, mostly men, clearly waiting to order something that wasn't on the menu.

Heartbroken at such an openly accepted cultural phenome-non, we left. That's when we noticed the row of taxis lined up outside along the street. We noticed that many of the working girls were either getting into or out of the cabs, sometimes paus-ing to chat with the drivers. Whenever a new customer came along, the driver was clearly inquiring if their passenger was interested in what the girls were offering. I couldn't believe it! The scenes that had seemed so safe and normal on our way down—the beach, fast-food shops, taxis—were now part of another, alien world, one where children were sexual commodities to be bought and sold, used and discarded.

My heart was shattered.

BREAKING BREAD OVER BULLETS

The next morning, after a much-needed night's sleep, we woke up and prepared to meet with a group of local pastors who wanted to take us to lunch and show us around the city. After introductions and greetings, we shared our experiences from the previous evening and learned that we had witnessed one of the city's greatest problems firsthand.

I had read somewhere that Fortaleza was second only to Thailand for sex trafficking but didn't realize just how widespread and overt it was in the culture. Apparently, Fortaleza was known to cater to sex tourists, offering a buffet of perverse pleasures for their warped desires. The sex trade was big business and commonly accepted by most residents as something that couldn't be changed.

Treating us as honored guests, our hosts took us to a very upscale restaurant. With beautiful colors and décor, the place looked modern and chic as we walked in. That is, until a uniformed guard greeted us with an Uzi submachine gun in hand! Protected by a bulletproof vest, this giant of a man questioned our hosts before nodding and waving us through to be seated. The local pastors were clearly familiar with such extreme security measures, but I couldn't get my jaw off the floor. There we were, in one of the most elegant restaurants in the city, and yet it had to be protected by an armed guard with an Uzi. We definitely were not in Nebraska anymore!

After a delicious and incident-free lunch, our hosts drove us to see the piece of property they had just purchased. They explained it was in the middle of the city's *favela*, a slum-ridden area inhabited by the homeless, addicts, criminals, and squatters. The area was crowded with shanties and makeshift camps and ruled by drug lords and their gangs. Crime-ridden and dangerously violent, the *favela* basically operated like an anarchy because the police considered it too dangerous to patrol. You know you have a problem when the *police* won't patrol a neighborhood because it's too dangerous!

As we drove along the slum's streets, our hosts told us that roughly a third of Brazil's urban population lives in a *favela*, most of them fatherless—which reveals how the cycles of poverty and crime continually perpetuate and enslave millions. People with blank stares and haunted eyes stopped to watch us, probably wondering why in the world we were there. The houses we passed had obviously been vandalized, with broken windows and graffiti-covered exteriors. Businesses no longer attempted to operate, leaving impromptu entrepreneurs to sell their wares on the sidewalks.

The place looked like a battle zone with dirt lots and broken concrete, but nonetheless these pastors had purchased land and established a church there. They held services every Friday night, with often as many as a hundred kids showing up. Our hosts also learned the hard way that they were not welcome there. Not wanting to haul musical instruments and their electronic equipment back and forth, they had purchased and installed a huge locker-like container on the property. The very first night it was there, the locker was broken into, robbed, and tagged with gang graffiti. Only empty beer cans and drug paraphernalia remained.

Despite this story and the urban decay of our desolate surroundings, I wasn't afraid. Our group was small, with five women and two men, but I had been in other *favelas* in Sao Paulo, as well as similar areas in the world's major cities. I figured our hosts would never have brought us there if any real danger existed, so I was just listening and silently praying, asking God to protect them and bless their ministry to the broken people of this community.

Probably the other reason I didn't feel endangered was because we were only going to take a quick look and leave. In fact, our hosts had left the cars unlocked so we could just get out, see the property, snap a few pictures on our phones, and hop back in again. There were people across the street, a little baby in just a diaper running around, a couple of shacks, and kids out playing and laughing. Then farther down the block from us, the only local within shouting distance was someone our hosts recognized as a man who regularly attended their Friday-night services. They exchanged greetings and again, no one seemed nervous or alarmed. The local guy nodded and grinned before taking a few steps away and getting out his phone, presumably to make a call.

As our hosts finished telling us about their vision for the church they had planted there, I praised God and was so excited for what they were doing.

Then, as we headed back to our car, I looked up and saw this young man—the same one who had called out to our hosts moments ago—running toward us and fumbling with something beneath a green-and-white checkered scarf.

It was a gun.

GRACE AT GUNPOINT

We must have looked like the fattest sitting ducks he had ever seen. There we were, with purses, watches, rings, and iPhones all on display. I had already heard that smartphones often sold for a thousand dollars or more there, but still it didn't occur to me to keep my phone out of sight. So this guy, who had been friendly one moment, was now very unfriendly, pointing a Glock at us.

He began to yell in Portuguese, and I didn't need a translator to know what he said. We were clearly being robbed! I felt frozen in place and was thankful when one of the other female pastors placed her arms around my shoulders. I was not alone. We were all together, and God was with us.

Then, seemingly out of nowhere, five or six other guys, many of them masked with kerchiefs or pieces of cloth over the lower halves of their faces, jumped out waving their guns at us too.

Now forgive me for this, but I immediately, almost without thinking, slipped off this ring I love to wear when I travel. I've had it for a while and it goes with almost everything, so it's perfect for traveling. It's actually the first ring my husband gave me, a temporary engagement ring while he was having my "real" ring designed and made. As much as I love my real ring, I'm hesitant to wear it when I travel, which is why I had this ring on instead.

Forget my purse; I'm not giving up my traveling ring quite so fast! Maybe it's the ghetto in me, but I slipped that ring off and tucked it into my pocket as fast as I could. As if my pocket were a secure hiding place for a band of robbers in the slums of Brazil.

One of them must have seen me, though, because he immediately came over and pointed at my pocket with his gun. That was about the same moment when I realized that maybe they weren't going to rob us—maybe they were going to hold us for ransom. Wow. There was nothing hopeful running through my mind in that instant. So in comparison to being kidnapped and tortured, giving up my jewelry wasn't a big deal at all!

I pulled out my beloved traveling ring, and the robber motioned for me to keep going. At the same time I was handing over my watch, my wedding ring, my phone, and my purse, I realized the rest of our group was facing the same fate. That's probably about the time I finally started praying and hoping they would just take our stuff and leave us alone. I knew enough about the Brazilian economy to know that the cash, gadgets, and jewelry they pulled off us would probably equal a year's salary for someone in the *favela*.

Just then Pastor Fernanda, a lovely Brazilian woman and one of our hosts, barked something at the gunman standing in front of Teena. Apparently, he had been trying to remove her necklace when Fernanda snapped and told him to back away, which he did, surprising us all.

And I remember thinking, *Lord, You're still God, You're still big, and You're right here with us.* Maybe it would all be over soon and we could just put it behind us and get on with our ministry. Just then, I looked over and saw the gunmen motioning for my friend Jodi and the rest of us to get on the ground.

It wasn't over yet.

BETRAYED BY BLOOD

Lying facedown on the sandy ground littered with cigarette butts and bottle caps and red stinging ants, I never allowed myself to think about what might happen, about the life-or-death danger we faced. I know now this was surely the Holy Spirit guarding my mind and heart, providing me with God's peace in a very unpeaceful setting.

But later I did think about what it must have been like for our hosts. While they knew we were venturing into a dangerous area to see their new property, they had recognized the guy who would rob us as someone from their services. Without knowing what they said, I could tell they had a friendly exchange. Facing betrayal by someone you trust is nothing new—it's as old as Cain taking the life of his brother Abel and Judas kissing Jesus to identify Him for the Roman guards. But later, as I reflected on people of faith in the face of danger, I thought of Joseph.

Joseph was probably shocked to learn just how much his brothers despised him. Maybe their father did show him a bit more favor than he showed his siblings, but surely they knew how much their father loved each of them. Of course, there was that bright rainbow patchwork coat—and that did make Joseph feel special.

And I'm guessing it wasn't just that colorful coat that made him feel special. Joseph was convinced that God had special things in store for him. Maybe Joseph would be a mighty warrior. Maybe he would travel to distant lands and mingle with kings and queens. Whatever great events waited on him ahead, Joseph knew they were coming because he kept having dreams. Strange and symbolic, these dreams indicated that he would someday be a great leader whom others would serve and revere.

One in particular spelled this out clearly. In this dream Joseph saw himself atop a hill that rose high above the rest of the earth, so high he could almost touch the clouds. From this height, he watched as the sun, the moon, and the stars gathered at his feet, bowing before him. Then there was the dream in which he and his brothers were binding sheaves of wheat out in the fields. Only, his sheaf of wheat suddenly rose up out of his hands while those of his brothers fell down before it.

Apparently, his brothers would one day bow before him.

But like most siblings, they didn't like hearing about these kinds of dreams from their younger brother. Maybe it was naive on Joseph's part to think that they would like hearing how much greater than them he would be. After all, they were already jealous of him! Why would they want to hear about how he would one day reign over them?

And it's funny, because even Jacob, Joseph's father, questioned whether these dreams were getting out of hand. Joseph was his favorite, but still, enough is enough. Like any good parent trying to keep peace in the family, Jacob basically told his son, "Look, do you really think your family will ever bow down before you? You're no king! Enough foolishness—get back to work!"

But apparently Jacob's attempt was unsuccessful. Because Joseph's brothers soon conspired to betray him. They were sick and tired of him and his dreams and decided to put an end to him once and for all.

> Now when they saw him afar off, even before he came near them, they conspired against him to kill him. Then they said to one another, "Look, this dreamer is coming! Come therefore, let us now kill him and cast him into some pit; and we shall say, 'Some wild beast has devoured him.' We shall see what will become of his dreams!" (Gen. 37:18–20 NKJV)

Can you imagine having your own family turn on you this way? Having a stranger threaten you is one thing, but from your own brothers it had to sting worse. Have you found yourself in the bottom of one of life's pits because of the way others treated you? In those scary moments, whether faced with a life-threatening situation or imprisoned by pain and loneliness, our faith often feels powerless. And sometimes, just like Joseph, we end up going from one pit to another. You may recall, his brothers didn't abandon him in that dry well—instead they sold him to some traveling foreigners, a group of Ishmaelites, who took him to Egypt. And if being sold into slavery wasn't bad enough, Joseph was falsely accused by his boss's wife and sent to jail.

Still, he never gave up.

HOLDING ON TO HOPE

I pray you've never been betrayed and put in danger like Joseph, but as a pastor, I'm often witness to the devastating consequences of adultery, abuse, and addiction. I know that many of us must deal with unexpected betrayals that harm us both emotionally and physically. I've seen the bruises on the faces of suburban housewives suffering domestic abuse in silence, and I've witnessed the horrors of children being sold into sex trafficking. I know violence does not discriminate.

Sometimes these moments of fearful danger may seem even tougher because you're trying to do the right thing. It's one thing to have others turn on you when you're being arrogant or acting like you're special, as Joseph may have. But it's another when you're trying to minister, to serve, to live out your God-given purpose. I mean, there we were in Brazil, ministering at the invitation of other believers and visiting the site of their new church when we were robbed at gunpoint!

Have you ever been robbed or had someone threaten or bully you so they could take what belonged to you? Have you had to endure threats and persecution from others in order to keep your dream alive? Betrayal comes in many forms. Like Joseph, maybe you have family members who remain jealous or harbor grudges. Or it could be coworkers or embittered team members willing to lie, cheat, and steal from you in the office. Perhaps your betrayal comes at the hands of people you thought were your friends, only to discover they've been assassinating your reputation with gossip on social media.

As painful, fearful, and desperate as those times may seem, you must never lose hope. Even in adverse circumstances, Joseph never gave up on God, and consequently he continued to experience the Lord's favor. Remaining faithful, Joseph refused to become a victim, and I suspect he didn't feel sorry for himself. Despite the painful wounds he suffered from his family and others around him, he knew God had not and would not abandon him. We must do the same, even when our world crashes around us and those we love betray us.

When we live by faith and trust God to heal our wounds and redeem our losses, it doesn't matter how deep the pit is or how frightening the situation feels. Even in our scariest moments, God still blesses us and brings us into the safety of His arms. We're told, "The LORD blessed the household of the Egyptian because of Joseph. The blessing of the LORD was on everything Potiphar had, both in the house and in the field" (Gen. 39:5).

I pray you're never thrown in a pit like Joseph or robbed at gunpoint like I was in Brazil, but nonetheless, you will still face hostility and adversity from others in your life. During those encounters, you may find yourself flat on the ground and feeling overwhelmed. But never give up! No matter how bleak or dangerous the situation, God is still there with you. He will not abandon you or forsake you. And when He is for you, it doesn't matter who is against you.

TALKING BACK

There on the ground in one of the worst parts of Fortaleza, I felt like Joseph must have felt at the bottom of his dry well. Being robbed was bad enough, but being robbed while I had no idea what our assailants were saying sure felt worse. Taking our cue from our hosts, my team remained on the ground.

Then I realized Pastor Fernanda wasn't lying down. She had started to kneel and then frozen in place. Suddenly, she began yelling at this gang of robbers, her syllables sharp and insistent, and I didn't need to understand Portuguese to know that she was letting them have it. It was like she had turned into the daughter of Wonder Woman and the Incredible Hulk! She almost scared me more than the robbers scared me in that moment. I prayed she would just shut up and be quiet—before these bandits got upset and retaliated.

The ringleader looked back at her while the other gang members went through our stuff, emptying wallets, comparing phones, and organizing the loot they had just taken from us. That was when I remembered the cars were unlocked, and I thought, *They're going to take our cars! Of course, they are. Or if they don't, then we'll be on our own in the* favela.

Talk about a bad situation becoming worse!

Meanwhile, Fernanda continued to yell at the gang leader. He waved his gun toward her, but still she angrily talked back to him. The tension escalated between them, and I couldn't understand why she was taking such a strong stand with no weapon or bargaining power. Did she lose sight of where we were and who we were facing? Was this a stress reaction she couldn't control?

Later, I found out what Fernanda was going on about. In the *favelas*, there's an unspoken code that dictates a certain respect for fellow inhabitants. It's one thing to rob tourists or the lost city dweller, but most of the time, people who lived in the *favela* left each other alone and tried to give each other a wide berth. It was sort of like, "Hey, we're from the same hood and know some of the same peeps, so I won't mess with you if you don't mess with me."

So Fernanda was telling these guys, "Look, we are not outsiders! I'm from here and belong here. We bought land here and started a church here—yes, a *church*! We've established a presence here in your community and we're staying. And this is how you think you can treat us? Are you crazy? This is terrible—you're breaking the rules. So stop it right now and let us go."

There on the ground I continued to pray in the Spirit. I didn't even have words, but I poured out my heart to God and asked Him to intervene, to show mercy, to protect me and my team and our hosts. I'm so glad that in those times of great stress and trauma, even when we don't know what to say or how to say it, we can still open ourselves to Him. He hears the cries of our hearts, and He surely heard mine that day.

So there I was, lying on the ground and praying like an original apostle at Pentecost, waging spiritual warfare against our captors and begging my heavenly Father to intervene in this situation. All without words—because Fernanda was surely using enough words for all of us! I had no idea what was about to happen, but I knew God had not abandoned us and was doing something in our midst right there, right then.

And still Fernanda kept talking and yelling at our captors.

Time felt as if it were moving in slow motion, and I have no idea how long we remained in place. It felt like a lifetime, and ultimately it doesn't matter how long we were there, because it was long enough. Long enough for God to hear our prayers and save our lives.

The armed robbers ran away.

Whatever Fernanda said to them—not to mention God— obviously worked. They took what they wanted and disappeared down the nearest alleyway. As we slowly stood up, I said, "Thank You, Jesus!" and soon everyone joined in, and we began having a major worship service. Then suddenly in the midst of all these hallelujahs, I said, "Uh, we should go now! Let's get in the car, okay?"

Just about to get in our car, I noticed something on the ground nearby. My purse lay unopened where it had fallen after the robber had taken it from me. While he could easily have placed the strap over his head, he must have dropped it when he needed to free up his hands to hold his gun along with more of our stuff.

All was not lost.

SAFELY HOME

We were about to drive away when Fernanda insisted we call the police to catch our thieves. Her husband was still sweating and shaking from our near-death encounter, like the rest of us, but this feisty woman remained furious about the situation.

"They won't get away with this! I'm calling the police, so get ready for a shootout!" she said. Apparently, anytime the police dared to venture into the *favela*, the result was a shootout between residents and the law enforcement officers. The gang leaders and drug lords considered it a personal offense for the police to enter their territory and made it known they would try to kill any police who showed up on their turf. But Fernanda didn't care— she wanted justice.

"It's okay, Fernanda," I said. "I don't need my watch or rings back—they can be replaced. Let's just get back to the church and put this behind us."

We compromised and let the men stay to talk to the police while the ladies returned to wait at our hosts' church. I must've been in shock because the rest of that day is a hazy blur. It was like I was in a movie! I started out on a plane in Omaha and ended up on the set of *Taken*!

Later that afternoon, the police called the church and told us they had identified the assailants who robbed us, thanks to a GPS device in one of our stolen iPhones. They now wanted us to come down to the police station and identify the guys they had arrested. Along with everyone else (well, except Fernanda, who became my hero that day), I was so traumatized that I didn't care—I just wanted to move on. Since we didn't want to press charges, the police let the guys go.

Fortunately, the rest of the trip was less eventful—well, not quite, but I'll tell you more about the other incident that happened in the next chapter. When we finally left Fortaleza, we were all talking about the trip and sharing the latest details learned about the thieves. Although no one had told me at the time, I learned that the police considered us extremely fortunate to be alive. Apparently, the gang that attacked us had a reputation for murdering their victims! No wonder my sister-in-law Teena waited to tell me until we were on the plane to leave—because I probably wouldn't have stayed had I known that. Well, maybe I would have stayed, but it wouldn't have been easy.

But God had protected us. He kept us safe in the palm of His hand. No matter what, He is a big God—the biggest—and will see you safely home. Thank You, Jesus!

SHIFTING RED MOMENTS TO GREEN TRIUMPHS

GO DEEPER

When have you faced a dangerous situation that left you worried about being harmed or injured? How did you handle your fears during that trial? How did you experience God through that scary circumstance? Who has betrayed you whom you need to forgive? What do you need to do in order to move on from the way they wounded you? Are you willing to invite God into the pain of the wound they caused in your life?

GO FURTHER

God,

I'm sure there have been so many times when You have protected me and I wasn't aware of the danger around me. Thank You for those times as well as the moments when I've been terrified by events beyond my control and the choices of other people.

When others betray me or manipulate me, seek revenge, or try to steal what is mine, allow me to forgive them, to show them the same mercy You show me on a daily basis.

As I continue to grow in my faith and draw closer to You, give me Your strength and power to confront my fears, regardless of their source. Remind me of Your loving protection and keep me safe in Your arms, Lord.

In Jesus' name, amen.

CHAPTER 9

THROW OUT
THE LIFELINE

REDEFINING RED WHEN
YOU'RE BOLD

Do not pray for tasks equal to your powers.
Pray for powers equal to your tasks.

—PHILLIPS BROOKS

B elieve it or not, I went to another sketchy neighborhood while visiting Fortaleza, Brazil. Even after being robbed there by a gang of Uzi-wielding young men, I returned to another unsafe area unafraid. I know; it sounds crazy, right? Why would I go back into this terrible, violent neighborhood where our group had been attacked at gunpoint only a couple of days earlier?

The only answer I can give is that it was because of the

children. And because of God, of course. He is always the source of true boldness, power, and the courage necessary to walk by faith and not fear. Despite the scary drama we'd experienced earlier, I felt remarkably calm and confident the rest of our trip. God had come through in amazing ways, just as He always did, and so when our hosts asked if we wanted to visit a government-funded safe house in the *favela*, we didn't hesitate to say yes.

My sister-in-law Teena, our friend Jodi, and I learned that the number of homeless kids and runaway teens in the city was staggering but almost impossible to calculate. And many of them, of course, were raised in the *favelas*. In fact, we were told that it was not uncommon for some parents to *sell* their children in order to pay their debts. Yes, you read that correctly! No one freaks out or calls child services or does anything at all. They're like, "Oh, that's a shame. Too bad."

Can you imagine talking to another woman and asking, "Hey, how's your little girl doing? How's Becky?" only to have the woman say, "Well, I don't know. I had to sell her to pay some bills this month." Please forgive me if that little exchange sounds glib, but I just couldn't—and still can't—wrap my mind around this practice being anything close to normal.

Unwanted children are also abandoned in the *favela*. We heard about one little baby boy left in a shoe box in a vacant lot in one of the most desperate parts of Fortaleza. Someone found him and took him home with them so they could groom him to be prostituted as soon as he could walk. It's horrifying, but it's real.

Government leaders don't even know the true number of people who live in *favelas* because they can't get in there to do the populous count. They guesstimate, so when people go missing, there's no search or questioning of suspects because most of the time there's no record that such a person even exists.

This safe house was supposed to be making a difference, but we quickly learned that it was likely only making the problem worse.

DIAMOND IN THE DARK

This safe house we visited was supposedly only for females who had run away or whose families had abandoned them. The manager, however, an older lady from the *favela*, was never on the premises. Instead, a scruffy team of adult men oversaw these girls, teens, and young women, rotating twenty-four-hour shifts. And if you're thinking this setup sounds like the foxes were guarding the hen house, then you would be absolutely right.

In addition to the absent matron, the place also had two "den mother"–type women who were supposed to teach the girls how to cook and clean so they could learn job skills. Because of the predatory men hanging around, however, these two ladies usually locked themselves in their respective rooms, one in the kitchen and the other in the office supply room.

These older women were there to teach, mentor, and influence the girls in a positive way but were terrified to do their jobs because they might be raped or sold. If they tried to resist or change the system, they would probably incite violence and they might be killed along with the girls and those they cared about. Yet this is where these young girls had to *live*.

It was a horrible situation all the way around.

When we questioned our hosts on how we could help change this place, we were told that our boldness in coming there to visit made a huge impact. We were showing both the girls and the people watching that followers of Jesus were not afraid to go into dark places and shine the light of God's love.

And as we pulled up to the gate, I knew right away this was indeed a dark place. I turned to the ladies in our team and quietly said, "There's something terribly wrong here. My spirit already feels heavy with grief before we even go in."

Waiting for someone to open the gate, we sat there for about ten minutes, wondering, praying, and anticipating with dread what waited for us on the other side.

While we waited, a dozen or more girls slowly began to surround our car. Ranging from elementary-school age to teens, they weren't talking or smiling—just warily sizing us up and wondering why we were there. I understood why these girls had trust issues with strangers, but it weighed on me that these precious souls looked like they might never trust anyone for the rest of their lives.

My sense of the place was further confirmed as we got out of the car and went inside. It was so desolate—it was hard to believe this was a government-funded institution offering hope and healing. The dry, dirt-packed ground was bare. Scraps of paper and litter blew through the courtyard.

Shuddering despite the heat, I felt as if we were going into the darkest of prisons. Was it Dante's *Inferno* that had "Abandon all hope, ye who enter here" inscribed over the gates of hell? While this place was supposed to be a place of hope, it sure didn't appear that way. I was grateful our team could bring the source of all hope, the Lord Jesus Christ, to shine like a bright diamond in this oppressive darkness.

Although the interior was clean and immaculate, it felt clinical and institutional. From the colorful bedspreads and pillows, it was clear some attempts had been made to brighten the rooms. Each girl had a cubbylike area and her own locker. I noticed each space included something personal and valuable to a particular girl. For one it was a sticker book, while another had a photograph of a family member or loved one. Others had stuffed animals or some other childhood souvenir.

The only windows were perched high near the ceiling and offered little natural light. As we proceeded into the shadows, the girls kept their distance despite our hosts' attempts to explain our hearts were for them. No host or guide emerged to show us around, so we just kept wandering through the structure, taking it all in.

Eventually we walked into one room where several men sat, murmuring among themselves before staring back at us. Once again, our hosts tried to explain who we were and the purpose of our goodwill visit. Then one of the men stood up and began following us, followed by a couple of others, and it became clear that they didn't want us alone with any of the girls, presumably because of what the girls might tell us. They didn't want to be exposed for what they were doing, so they were making sure they hovered around to intimidate the girls and keep an eye on us.

They kept following us, and one of them totally creeped me out. My skin was crawling like this guy was the Devil, and the environment felt so heavy and dark around him, like a black cloud over his head. Noticing my discomfort, my friend Jodi said, "What's the deal with that guy? Are you okay?"

"I don't know," I whispered back. "I just can't stand being close to him because it's uncomfortable."

Later one of our hosts told us that particular guy was a known Devil worshipper. No wonder I felt weird, right? When light and darkness collide, there's always friction, a storm front in the making. I began praying for that place and those girls, and I'm not sure I've stopped since then.

Gradually, the girls began talking, shyly, and our hosts translated their questions. As we interacted with them, we learned some of them had attended outreaches our hosts had organized nearby. Many of them had been healed of various ailments there, including one little girl's brain cancer. Another girl, who we learned suffered from schizophrenia, seemed very curious about us, so we sat down and prayed with her.

As we finished our prayer and stood up, she said something in Portuguese that, when translated, broke my heart: "Oh, so you're leaving? Yeah, of course you are."

In her tearful eyes I could read volumes behind her resigned words of desperation. She seemed to say, "You people act like you care, but do you really? So many people come and go here, but nothing ever changes. It will always be this way."

We were all so moved by her implicit plea that we sat down again and began talking some more through our translator. One thing led to another, and about a half hour later, this little girl prayed to receive Jesus into her heart! We made sure she understood that while people might come and go and disappoint her in life, Jesus would always be there for her. I still think about the transformation on her face, turning her grim, tight expression into an open smile. The kind of change that only comes from experiencing God's love.

ONE LOST SHEEP

Moving deeper into the building, we encountered another girl, probably around fifteen, with short orange hair. Talking with her, we learned that most of the girls were allowed to return home—if they had one—for the weekend before returning during the week. She had just returned but revealed she really didn't have a home because her father was in prison and her mother had disappeared. So she used the time on the weekend to turn tricks and make money. *It was what she had done for as long as she could remember.*

"There are other things you can do," I said. "You don't have to keep living this way."

She watched us, smiling, as our host interpreted: "Oh, I won't always live this way—I have a dream! Someday I will be a powerful drug dealer and quit working the streets. I will leave the *favela* and charge men a lot of money and we'll meet in fancy hotels!"

Just when I didn't think my burdened heart could feel any heavier, this young woman told us her dream in life was to deal drugs and be a high-class prostitute. While I hurt for her, I didn't judge her and I understood her rationale. She had no family, no education, so what else did she have to work toward?

"Why did you come here?" she asked, as we continued talking. "Why are you here?"

"You mean in Fortaleza?" I asked.

"No," she said, shaking her head and pointing down. "I mean, right *here*." It was like she couldn't imagine why anyone would choose to enter this place and visit where we now stood. And while it was clear why most people would not want to venture into such a building in such a neighborhood, I also knew their reluctance only made the need greater for those living there.

"I came here all the way from Omaha, Nebraska, in the United States," I explained. "I left my home to come here and tell you that somebody loves you and believes you're important. You are so valuable! You have a hope and a destiny and a future."

"You came all the way from there, just for me?" She looked up at me and began to cry.

"Yes, I did."

And I meant it. If I went on that trip to Brazil for no one else, if I had survived that robbery for no other reason, I knew in that moment I went there for her. As our hosts continued our tour, this young lady followed me and held my hand. She clung to me and walked beside me, telling the other girls we encountered, "This is my friend! This is my new friend!"

Once I knew what she was saying, I began to interrupt her and say, "No, no—this is *my* new friend! She's my friend!" And that would make her smile, which, of course, made me smile too.

Even knowing all I know about Fortaleza, I'm more than willing to return—in fact, I went not long ago. Through the loving boldness of God's Spirit, I will continue to illuminate the darkness. Because I know even in the most confusing, devastating situations, God is there. Like the good shepherd leaving his flock of ninety-nine to find the one lost sheep, He will never give up on us.

THE CUSP OF CHAOS

Visiting that "safe" house in the slums of Fortaleza reminded me of another young woman's story in the Bible, someone not unlike most of these girls who sold their bodies to survive. Identified as Rahab the harlot, she found herself thrust into a situation that not only required strength and courage—it required boldness. In order to save herself as well as her family, she had to take an incredible leap of faith. Rahab had to trust foreigners she had never met, but more important, she had to trust their God with all she had—her heart, her life, her loved ones. But the result of her boldness was more than she could have imagined.

Rahab's story occurred on the cusp of chaos as the Israelites, after wandering for forty years in the desert, were finally entering the promised land, led by Joshua since Moses had just passed away (see Joshua 1 for the full story). First stop: the walled city of Jericho, our girl Rahab's hometown. Obeying God's instructions, Joshua secretly sent two spies into Jericho to get the lay of the land and report back to him.

These two men, who would obviously be killed if discovered, knocked on Rahab's door and asked for refuge. She took them in, hid them under some stalks of flax she had drying on her roof, and then lied to the king's messenger, who was inquiring because word had spread of the imminent attack. Basically, she pointed to the city gate and misdirected the king's men by saying, "They went that way!"

Think about this for a moment. It's one thing to harbor foreign spies in your home, but it's another altogether to outright lie about it to your leader. That kind of boldness took guts! For that dramatic deception, Rahab had to be either untrustworthy and disloyal by nature, or willing to trust in something and someone greater than her act of treason.

We can't know what was going on inside Rahab before that moment, but I suspect God must have already been knocking at her heart's door long before she heard the spies at the door of her home. Maybe He sent others ahead to plant seeds before the harvest occurred in that moment of bold choices and dangerous decisions. Because instead of turning away these two foreign spies and the danger they brought to her house, she welcomed them and gave them a hiding place. God may have caused a dramatic acceptance in her heart—He surely could cause such a miraculous transformation—but from my experience, boldness often emerges from our past obedience and faithfulness.

Have you faced a situation similar to Rahab's when you felt trapped between a rock and a hard place? Perhaps you faced a knock on your door in the form of a doctor's dire diagnosis or your boss's backstabbing. Or maybe you're faced with enforcing strong boundaries with loved ones who are addicts or with abusive family members. No matter the form, we all face these dilemmas when we feel trapped.

Which means there's only one choice: to follow God.

WHEN A RED CORD MEANS GO

Sometimes what appears to be a dangerous situation might actually be the means by which God delivers His mercy. The girls who prayed to know Jesus in that grungy safe house in the *favela* might not have met Him if they had not been in that terrible place at that divinely appointed time. Of course, God would have continued pursuing them and penetrating their lives in other ways. But out of the darkest situation you or I might be able to imagine, God's light shone as a bright beacon of His love and hope to those girls.

Like Rahab hearing the knock at her door, we, too, must follow the Lord, trusting His direction for our lives, even when it goes against logic and loyalty. Based on her example, the direct approach of looking boldly into the face of danger and darkness provides a way forward. This doesn't mean we won't be afraid, alarmed, or anxious. I wonder if Rahab second-guessed the bold choice she made while standing in her doorway and delivering an Oscar-worthy performance. Because right after deceiving the king's men, she went up to the roof to have a cards-all-on-the-table talk with the two men she had just saved. Let's take a look.

Before the spies lay down for the night, she went up on the roof and said to them, "I know that the LORD has given you this land and that a great fear of you has fallen on us, so that all who live in this country are melting in fear because of you. . . . Now then, please swear to me by the LORD that you will show kindness to my family, because I have shown kindness to you. Give me a sure sign that you will spare the lives of my father and mother, my brothers and sisters, and all who belong to them—and that you will save us from death."

"Our lives for your lives!" the men assured her. "If you don't tell what we are doing, we will treat you kindly and faithfully when the LORD gives us the land." (Josh. 2:8–9, 12–14)

151

Here we see that Rahab was not only bold, she was also smart. She had heard about what their God had done for them—parting the Red Sea so they could escape from Egypt, sustaining them for many years, and empowering them to conquer formidable tribes in the area. I can almost see the wheels turning in that moment when she asked the spies to make her a divine deal. She clearly believed what she had heard about the mighty things their God had done—or if she didn't fully believe them yet, she was certainly intrigued and willing to risk her life and the safety of her family on it. Maybe Rahab was a gambler at heart, but this kind of wager was all or nothing.

Owing her a debt of gratitude for hiding them, and perhaps impressed with her bold courage under pressure, the spies did indeed seal the deal she requested. They told her that they would return in three days with the full force of the Hebrew army behind them to destroy the city walls of Jericho and claim it as their own. In order to ensure her safety, they instructed her to hang a red cord out her window as a signal that she and her family were to be spared once that battle began.

The conquest of Jericho went down just as the spies told her it would. (You can check it out in Joshua 6.) Rahab obeyed their instructions, lowered the red cord from her window, and she and her family were indeed saved—in fact, they were the only ones! In her case, red *really* meant go. And Rahab's story not only had a happy ending—it had an epic impact on the Christian faith. Because she was not only an ancient-world Wonder Woman; Rahab went on to be a direct ancestor of Jesus Himself!

You see, Rahab became the mother of Boaz (who married a widow you might recall named Ruth), and Boaz fathered Obed, and then Obed was the dad of Jesse, who was the father of David, the shepherd boy anointed by God to be king. From David there came Solomon, whose son Rehoboam had a son named Abijah, and from him the genealogical torch was passed to Jehoshaphat, and down through many more generations until we get to a certain carpenter from Nazareth named Joseph—the husband of Mary and earthly father of God's only Son, Jesus!

Yes, the fact that the Savior of the world, the Messiah, came through the lineage of a woman known to have been a harlot back in Jericho was considered scandalous. But it is undeniable! Not only is Rahab included in Matthew's genealogy of Christ (Matt. 1:5), but she's also included in the "Faith Hall of Fame" found in Hebrews: "By faith the prostitute Rahab, because she welcomed the spies, was not killed with those who were disobedient" (Heb. 11:31). Maybe you or I wouldn't have chosen her as a logical or worthy choice, but God sure did!

Rahab remains a hero of faith for all of us who have made bad choices in our past or have been forced to overcome desperate circumstances. I can't imagine what those girls in that Brazilian safe house have endured or suffered through. But no matter what we've faced or what decisions we may regret, Rahab's story reminds us that we all have choices no matter how hard they may seem in the moment. If we're willing to seek God's direction and boldly follow Him and obey His Word, we will find the same deliverance and freedom Rahab discovered.

Thrust into the middle of a situation that felt inescapable, Rahab trusted the voice of God and went against what appeared logical or rational. And out of her faithfulness, it's clear that God had great plans for her and wanted to use her in a dramatic way to further His kingdom. He chose her—out of all the queens and princesses as well as countless other women of faith. God chose

Rahab the prostitute to be a mega-great-grandmother for His only begotten Son!

Even when we can't see it, even when circumstances obscure it or make it seem unlikely or improbable, God also has a plan for our lives. While you may struggle with doubt and wonder why you face certain trials in your life, you must never forget that God can redeem everything and use it for His good in our lives. "We know that in all things God works for the good of those who love him, who have been called according to his purpose" (Rom. 8:28).

As difficult as it can be to understand a culture where little girls are bought and sold, we must trust that God can and will deliver them—and all who are held captive by the powers of darkness in this world. And we are given an opportunity to assist in this process as we let our light shine. Just as Jesus' shed blood on the cross heals us, we can extend the red cords in our lives as lifelines of grace. Remembering how God rescued us and gave us new life is a wellspring of bold love like no other.

BOLD AND BELOVED

Reflecting on the way God empowers us to love boldly, I recall a time in my life when I was expecting God to do the miraculous. My maternal grandfather, who was not a Christian to our family's knowledge, was in hospice care and his doctors said he might die at any time. My mom had flown to Phoenix to be with him as his time was winding down. One particular morning my mom called to say that the nurses didn't think it would be much longer. This totally blew my mind because the Lord had just told me I was supposed to go there and give my granddad the opportunity to accept the Lord as his Savior.

While I was excited at this opportunity, I also felt it was a divine assignment from God. So I told my mom I was coming down and the next day arrived in Phoenix. The scorching temperatures reminded me of just how hot the desert gets. But nothing could deter me from my mission. The Lord had entrusted me with a very important assignment, and I had all our church's prayer warriors helping me. I just knew something amazing was about to happen.

When I arrived, however, I discovered my grandfather was experiencing very few moments of lucidity, and of course I needed him to be coherent to understand the conversation about salvation I hoped we could have. As the hours turned into days, I continued to pray for a window of time into his heart. Surely, I was not there in vain.

I was down to only two days left before I was scheduled to come home. I prayed, consistently asking the Lord to open a window and allow Grandpa to be able to understand who God really was. On the fourth day, that window opened. We got a call saying he was awake, alert, and very conscious of his surroundings. With my mother and two sisters, I rushed to the hospital. And there he was, waiting, smiling, and completely aware of who we were!

For more than half an hour, we reminisced and chuckled about family stories. Then our hearts seemingly stopped when suddenly my grandfather looked at my mom, his eldest daughter, and said, "Who are you?" We stared in amazement as we saw his disease manifest in front of us. Swiftly, my mom ushered us out, as she didn't want us to remember him this way.

Nurses immediately rushed in, and in that moment the Lord

told me that now was the time to talk about Him and pray with my grandfather. Of course, I knew it was the most inopportune moment and that the medical staff and my mother wouldn't allow me back in. Nonetheless, I knew this might be my only opportunity, so I leaned over to Mom and whispered, "I need to pray with Grandpa." My mother looked at me and saw that this wasn't a question; it was a statement. She told the lead nurse, who said they would settle him and then let me know when we could come back.

In that moment, I knew there was a war going on in the supernatural realm for my grandfather's eternity. I was fully aware that this was quite possibly his last opportunity to meet the King of the Universe, his Creator, and accept Him into his heart. I began to pace that hospital hallway, asking God to give my grandfather a moment of lucidity, to bring him to a clear mind, if only for a minute. As I was praying, a nurse popped her head out and said, "You can come in now."

When I went in, she suddenly had to go down the hall to get something. I smiled, loving how wonderfully God had cleared the path to this moment to talk about Him with my grandfather. Approaching Grandpa's bed, I prayed with great expectancy. The man that I recall being six foot two, strong, and muscular, lay before me looking frail and small. His thin frame looked so tired. I touched his arm gently and said, "Hey, Grandpa, it's me—Elictia." I left my hand on him.

"I know who you are, darling," he said, smiling, and opened his eyes. What a miracle! I couldn't believe this answer to my prayers was happening in front of me. I was screaming with excitement on the inside because in that precise moment, I knew the grandpa I remembered was lying right there. He was alert and aware of me and his surroundings.

I seized the moment. The Bible says, very simply, that if you believe in your heart that Jesus is the resurrected Savior and confess with your mouth that you believe in Him to forgive your sins, then you will be saved. With this in mind, I wanted him to repeat a prayer of salvation, but I didn't want him to just repeat what I was saying—I needed him to believe it, to mean it as his own.

Okay, God, I silently prayed. *I know You have brought me here for this moment. So now I am going to let You do the rest.* Just then I felt the Lord prompting me to begin to pray, so I did.

"Father, right now in the name of Jesus—"

"Hallowed be Thy name," said my grandfather.

It felt like another miracle! I hadn't intended to pray the Lord's Prayer with my grandpa, but I sensed I should follow his lead so I repeated, "Hallowed be Thy name."

"Thy kingdom come, Thy will be done," he continued, and I then repeated.

We said the entire Lord's Prayer with my voice echoing after his. Then I said to him, "Okay, Grandpa, now I'm going to pray, and if, and *only* if, you believe what I am praying, then repeat after me. Only pray it if you believe what I'm saying, okay?"

"Yes, yes, I understand, darling," he said, "only if I agree with you."

I then prayed a simple prayer of salvation. "I believe in my heart and am confessing with my mouth that God sent His Son, Jesus, to die on the cross for our sins, and then on the third day He rose from the dead so that whoever believes in Him shall not ever perish, but they will have eternal life."

My grandfather repeated this prayer in its entirety.

"In Jesus' name, amen," I prayed.

He nodded and said, "In Jesus' name, amen."

He repeated, "In Jesus' name, amen."

I smiled, and he smiled, and we basked in the glow of what had just transpired. But then he looked up at me and said, "Who are you?"

"Oh, just someone who will see you again in heaven," I said, with my eyes full of tears. "I love you, Grandpa. See you soon, sir." With that, I touched his arm, and walked toward the door of his room whispering under my breath, "Hallelujah!"

I remain fully convinced the Lord opened a porthole and allowed my grandfather to be coherent just long enough to establish where he would spend eternity. Boy, was I ecstatic! My hope and expectation had been that Grandpa would accept the Lord as his Savior, and on the other side of my expectation was my miracle. God had empowered me to be bold enough to face this opportunity directly, and He had honored His promise to be present.

Grandpa died a short time later. But even as I grieved his passing from this earth, I was still able to celebrate in my heart. Because God tells us that when we leave our earthly bodies, we are present with Christ and so therefore with God.

The source of our boldness remains in Him.

SHIFTING RED MOMENTS TO GREEN TRIUMPHS

GO DEEPER

We do not lose heart. Though outwardly we are wasting away, yet inwardly we are being renewed day by day. For our light and momentary troubles are achieving for us an eternal glory that far outweighs them all. So we fix our eyes not on what is seen, but on what is unseen, since what is seen is temporary, but what is unseen is eternal. (2 Cor. 4:16–18)

When have you been forced to make a bold decision in the midst of scary circumstances? How did God answer your prayers and meet you in those moments? How has God used the consequences of your boldness in the lives of others? Is there someone you need to speak to today, someone who needs to hear the gospel and accept Jesus as Lord? Spend a few minutes in prayer, asking God to direct you to the people and places where He wants to use you in bold ways for His kingdom.

GO FURTHER

Father,

I thank You for the many ways You boldly empower me through Your Spirit and Your Word.

So many times I get preoccupied with my fears and doubts, all the stress and anxiety caused by my circumstances. But I know You are the source of all peace, comfort, and joy—even in the midst of painful moments when I cannot see what You are doing. During those times, strengthen my faith so I can trust You just like Rahab did when she heard the knock on her door.

Help me not to fear confronting my problems but to rest in the comforting knowledge of Your mercy, sovereignty, and power. I love You, Lord.

In Jesus' name, amen.

CHAPTER 10

COMING HOME

REDEFINING RED WHEN YOU'RE LOVED

God loves each of us as if there
were only one of us.

—Saint Augustine

Sometimes red means go, even if you aren't sure where you're going or what you'll find there. That was my experience as I made the decision to switch gears in my career and focus on general news rather than professional sports. I was more than ready for a change of pace.

As my career as a broadcast journalist continued to flourish, I began to long for more than it could provide. Maybe it was just getting older and realizing in my thirties that constantly traveling and changing locations every two to three years consumed all my energy. Or more likely, it was simply the Lord preparing me for the next season of my life and the way I would meet my future husband and father of my children.

Whatever it was, I began to look for a job that not only would keep me in the United States but would provide me with regular hours and a more consistent schedule. I had been blessed to work for CNBC in Hong Kong and ESPN in Singapore. I had traveled around the world and watched my career path exceed anything I could have ever planned on my own. But I sensed God leading me in a new direction and realized that included settling down and thinking about my future.

I prayed this would include a husband and a family, but I wasn't sure.

MOVING TO THE MIDWEST

I had always hoped I would marry a true man of God someday but knew the demands of my job and frequent travel made that challenging. When you're working all over the world, it's tough to find the kind of man I hoped to meet. But I trusted God's timing and knew that when the time was right, He would bring the right man into my life, if indeed He wanted me to marry.

But that wasn't why I accepted a position in Omaha, Nebraska, as a morning anchor for KETV, the local ABC affiliate there. I took that job because I was ready to slow down and settle in to a community. Having seen some of the largest cities in the world, and having met and interviewed some of the most glamorous, successful people in those places, I knew I preferred something a little more grounded. As fun as it was to go to exotic

locales and mingle with pro athletes and celebrities, I was beginning to feel a little jaded.

I didn't know much about Omaha when I took the job, only
that it was home to about half a million residents and had a view-
ing market of about 1.5 million throughout its metropolitan
area. I knew it was the largest city in Nebraska and located on
the Missouri River and that it was home to Berkshire Hathaway,
the company owned by Warren Buffett, one of the richest
people in the world. I learned Omaha is home to Creighton, a
well-respected private Jesuit university. While Omaha has no
professional sports teams, it nonetheless has had a long history
of passionate fans, especially for collegiate athletics.

After making the move to the Midwest, I immediately
appreciated the warmth and hospitality of friendly faces and a
more relaxed, slower pace than the West Coast. I quickly settled
into my new job and enjoyed coanchoring *First News*, the morning news program for KETV. Once my boxes were unpacked
and I began to get settled, I immediately began looking for a
church home.

I knew this process could prove more challenging than
expected based on my past moves. In fact, by this point I had
developed a system to expedite the process since I didn't really
want to spend months visiting dozens of churches before finding the community of believers where the Lord wanted me to
contribute. My system was actually quite simple: after praying
fervently and asking God to guide me to where He wanted me to
be, I turned to the list of churches in the Omaha phone book's
Yellow Pages. Yes, this was before iPhones and Google became
our primary search tools.

Trusting the Lord to guide me, I would then work my way

down the alphabetized list of churches, calling and explaining that I was new to the community and looking for a church home. You would be surprised how much you can tell about a church just by talking to the receptionist or staff member answering the phone. I'm certainly not one to pass judgment, especially not based on a five-minute phone call, but still I trusted my instincts and listened for God's leading.

Most churches I called sounded nice enough, and I visited several. Then one lady I spoke to at one of these churches asked me if I knew about Eagle's Nest, which I hadn't heard of at that time. So a few days later I dialed Eagle's Nest Worship Center and chatted briefly with a lovely woman who seemed genuinely excited for me to visit and check them out. She described their beliefs, their style of worship, and the overall sense of Christian community she enjoyed there. I jotted down their service times and address, planning to attend their Wednesday night service that evening.

Little did I know I was not only about to find my church home, but I was also about to meet the man I would marry!

LANDING IN THE EAGLE'S NEST

Walking in to the Eagle's Nest sanctuary that night, I wasn't sure what to expect. I had persuaded a friend from work to accompany me, and as we walked in, he immediately recognized a woman standing in the choir whom he had interviewed for a story the week before. She recognized him and smiled a warm welcome as we found seats and prepared for the service to begin.

Unbeknownst to me at the time, my arrival caused quite a stir. Sometime later, after I became engaged to Jim Hart, the senior pastor there, I discovered that many of the Eagle's Nest faithful knew Jim and I would marry even before we started dating! Matthew Henson, the administrative pastor's son, told us that when I showed up that Wednesday evening, he leaned over to his mom and whispered, "There is the pastor's wife!" Another staff member, the woman leading the children's ministry, also received a message from the Lord about my future there. She heard God tell her to go and find the visitor because that newcomer was someone very special.

Later I would also discover that their responses were not typical when it came to the pastor. Since Jim's wife had passed away six years earlier, his flock had become fiercely protective of him and his reputation. They were wary of any "ministry groupie" looking for an opportunity to be in the spotlight as a pastor's wife. Plus, they knew and loved Jim and grieved his loss along with him. They wanted to protect his heart and make sure that no one came along to distract him from the powerful ministry he led at Eagle's Nest.

But apparently, many of them knew I was the one for their pastor and were willing to finally let their guard down. They not only lowered their wall of protection around their beloved pastor, they outright pushed us together! Obviously, I liked the spirit of the people at Eagle's Nest and sensed the presence of the Lord there; it felt like home. As I began attending more services and events and getting more involved, I would show up only to discover that the only seat available was next to Pastor Hart. Whether it was a new member's class or a potluck in the fellowship hall, everyone else had clearly conspired to make sure Jim and I got better acquainted.

Nonetheless, it didn't really help the situation. In fact, it was obvious that Jim and I both felt really awkward and didn't know how to interact with each other. I didn't want to be seen as some kind of distraction. And poor Jim, who was used to being in the public eye, didn't want to be seen as someone trying to hit on a member of his flock. Compounding the dynamic was the fact that we were both public figures in our communities. I was on everyone's TV for several hours each morning, while Jim was a well-known, highly respected leader in the city.

And truth be told, there wasn't any real chemistry between us yet. I didn't even get to hear him preach until I had attended several times. I can remember wondering, *Does their senior pastor even preach anymore?* Even after meeting him that first Wednesday night and later hearing him preach, I didn't feel an overwhelming attraction or sense that he would be my future husband. After all, I wasn't there to check out the pastor. He just seemed like a great guy whom everyone clearly respected and appreciated.

This uncomfortable dynamic even made me wonder if I should leave the church and try another. I remember calling my aunt, a pastor's wife herself back in Seattle, and explaining the situation to her.

"Yes, that does sound weird," she said. "I really think you should try to pray about your feelings."

After I did just that, the craziest thing happened: Jim asked me out.

FROM WEIRD TO WONDERFUL

Walking into the church classroom that evening, I immediately became aware that something was different. There was tension in the air. Along with several dozen others, I was there for a covenant membership class led by Pastor Hart.

Maybe it was just seeing him again after what had happened a couple of weeks earlier. Another church staff member, Pastor Brian, had invited me to join him and his wife in attending a car show. I agreed, only to meet them at the event center and discover that Brian had also invited Pastor Hart. So there we were once again, sitting awkwardly with an elephant in the room that everyone else seemed intent on feeding.

After the class ended and people were chatting and putting on their coats, Pastor Hart came over to me. He had a perplexed expression on his face, and I wondered what was wrong.

"Uh, hi, Elictia," he said. "Can I talk to you for a minute?"

"Hi, Pastor Hart," I said. "Yes, of course."

"Uh, I'm really glad you're becoming a member of our church," he said awkwardly.

I smiled politely, wondering what he really wanted.

"Yeah," he said. "Well, I'll just say it because I don't have any clue what I'm doing or how this should be done . . ." He shuffled awkwardly, looking over his shoulder to see if anyone else was listening before he continued. "I just want to ask for your phone number. I thought we could . . . well, I'll give you a call and, you know, we could grab a bite or something . . . I don't want you to feel put off or like you need to leave the church if you don't want to. I just . . . thought I'd ask."

I giggled at how nervous he was and gave him my number. Driving home that night, I remember feeling relieved and hoping that his initiative would end this weird tension one way or another. I didn't want to have to find a new church, but I was becoming intrigued with the prospect of learning more about Mr. Jim Hart.

Sure enough, he called me the next day and we made plans to go out. Because I often received free tickets to concerts, plays, and events at the TV station, I suggested we attend a show at the Rose Theater that weekend. He agreed and said we could have dinner before the show. As nervous as I was before that date, I was immediately put at ease by how relaxed Jim seemed when we met. There was no longer a weird static between us. Instead, we were just a man and woman enjoying each other's company.

Things moved rather quickly after that first date in January. Both of us clearly enjoyed getting better acquainted and sensed that God, not just His followers, might actually be up to something. Jim was easy to talk to and shared my passion for God and serving His kingdom. We were both ready for a change in our lives, open to where the Lord would lead us.

Which turned out to be the altar! By May, just about four months after our first date, Jim proposed and I accepted. Everyone at church was thrilled, of course. We had already talked about the subject of marriage, and I knew that for a pastor in his position, we would want to move quickly. But I also wanted time to plan the big wedding I'd been dreaming about since I was a little girl. With both factors in mind, we set the date for October and embarked on a new life together as husband and wife.

It's the best change I've ever made!

LOSING YOUR WAY

While I knew it was time for a change in my life, it didn't make the decision to move to Omaha or the hassles of moving any easier. And even though I knew I loved Jim and that God had brought us together, I still had those moments of uncertainty that occur when a person who has been single for a long time agrees to get married. These were wonderful changes in my life, but at first they were still a little scary.

No one enjoys the stress caused by making a major life change. Even when we know it's the right thing and what God wants us to do, leaving familiarity for uncertainty is hard.

As a result, many times in our lives we work hard to avoid change and the unsettling adjustments change requires of us. Switching careers, losing a loved one, going back to school to finish a degree, moving across country, getting married, having children—these milestones inherently cause us to adapt to new and very different circumstances.

During these transitions, we often find ourselves forced to rely on the Lord and to trust His leading. We may not understand the timing or be able to see our destination, but we nonetheless step out in faith to follow Him. It's not easy and never will be, but that's why it's so vitally important to remain anchored by God's love for us. No matter where we are in life, His love will always lead us home to Him.

This is especially important when we end up somewhere we never wanted to be. Maybe it's suffering an abusive relationship or battling an addiction, facing bankruptcy or losing our home. In these situations, we know we need to change but don't always know how to find the strength to risk a different path. Sometimes we even have to hit rock bottom before we can make a U-turn and head back home to our Father's open arms.

This is the way a young woman I know discovered the love of God. As I recall, she and her sister grew up on a farm in a rural community with loving parents committed to following the Lord. Like many adolescents, however, when the younger sister got older, she began to rebel and wanted to leave their farm for the allure and glamor of the big city.

Knowing she would one day inherit the valuable farmland with her sister, the younger girl told her parents she was leaving and demanded that they hand over her inheritance right then. Shocked and saddened, the girl's father saw there was no talking her out of her decision, so he withdrew a sizable amount from the bank and gave it to this entitled young woman who had once been his baby girl. It must have broken her parents' hearts to watch her leave.

And then, well, we both know what happened next, don't we? This young lady arrived in the city and went on a major shopping spree—Saks, Neiman Marcus, Coach, Gucci, Louis Vuitton, you name it. Dressed to the nines in her sexy new clothes and bling, she then hit all the hottest clubs and partied like never before. Everyone noticed her and seemed enthralled by her beauty, energy, and class.

Soon she had more friends than ever and hot men blowing up her phone night and day. With shopping, drinking, and partying consuming her time, she had no time to miss her family back on the farm or to consider her future. She also refused to slow down on her spending—that is, until it was too late. Within a few months, all the cash her dad had given her had slipped through her hands like a spilled drink at the bar.

Unable to get a job, she was forced to pawn all her bling and ask her friends for help. Unfortunately, though, her so-called friends all seemed to disappear. No one returned her calls or responded on social media. She was no longer invited to private parties and couldn't afford to go to the clubs where she once ruled. She could no longer pay her rent and soon found herself on the street. Destitute, desperate, and devastated, this young woman began sleeping on park benches or at homeless shelters. She would beg for change at intersections and scrounge through dumpsters behind fast-food joints looking for food.

One day, as she unwrapped a cold burger pulled from the dumpster, she came to her senses. "I can't believe I'm eating this!" she said to herself. "The animals back on the farm eat better than I'm eating!" As much as it pained her to swallow her pride, she decided she would go back and ask her father to give her a job on the farm. That way she would at least have a place to live and healthy food to eat.

So she began to save up the change and dollar bills people handed her until she had enough for a bus ticket. After traveling all day, she was even more tired and grimy, and the fact she hadn't showered in days didn't help. Still, she had no choice, so she started walking from the bus station toward the gravel road leading back to her family's farm.

And just as she rounded the corner and began trudging up the long driveway to the farmhouse, she looked up and saw someone running toward her. It was her father! And he was laughing and crying, shouting and yelling, rushing toward her until he wrapped her in his arms and held her close. Safe in his arms, she could keep back the tears no longer and sobbed on her daddy's shoulder, just like when she was a little girl.

"Oh, Daddy!" she said. "I'm so sorry . . ." The words choked in her throat as she began to cry again.

"Shh, it's okay, baby," her father whispered. "I thought you were dead. But here you have come home to me! I can't wait to celebrate!"

NO PLACE LIKE HOME

Forgive me for taking creative license with one of Jesus' best-known parables, but sometimes it helps if we can hear familiar stories in a fresh way. I'm guessing most of us have heard the story of the prodigal son found in Luke 15, but the dramatic reunion he experienced when he finally returned home almost always brings me to tears.

> While he was still a long way off, his father saw him and was filled with compassion for him; he ran to his son, threw his arms around him and kissed him.
>
> The son said to him, "Father, I have sinned against heaven and against you. I am no longer worthy to be called your son."
>
> But the father said to his servants, "Quick! Bring the best robe and put it on him. Put a ring on his finger and sandals on his feet. Bring the fattened calf and kill it. Let's have a feast and celebrate. For this son of mine was dead and is alive again; he was lost and is found." So they began to celebrate. (Luke 15:20–24)

As my fictional paraphrase points out, this story is all about the Father's love when His children go astray. Jesus told this story, along with parables about the lost sheep and the lost coin, to make a point to the Jewish religious leaders criticizing Him because of the way He mingled with sinners. He said, "I tell you that in the same way there will be more rejoicing in heaven over one sinner who repents than over ninety-nine righteous persons who do not need to repent" (v. 7).

The religious leaders were all about following the letter of the law and being as self-righteous as humanly possible. But Jesus made it clear that true change occurs in our hearts when we confess our sins and ask God to forgive us. When we face what we've done and humbly ask for mercy, our Father is quick to forgive and welcome us home.

Jesus made it clear that the Father's love has no limits and welcomes us home no matter what we've done or how badly we've messed up. I talk with so many women who feel ashamed of past decisions and youthful indiscretions. Some had abortions when they were young, while others have had affairs or embezzled money from work. Others may have made peace with their past but carry a cloud of shame around over the way they gossip about friends behind their backs or remain addicted to shopping to soothe their hearts.

But it doesn't matter what we've done or what we're currently battling. Jesus won the fight once and for all. God loved us so much He sacrificed the most precious thing He had—His only Son. Because Christ was willing to die on the cross for our sins, we are forgiven and can enjoy fellowship with God here on earth and later in heaven. But in order to experience the fullness of His love and the many good gifts He wants to give us, we must remain open and obedient.

We must be willing to realize that sometimes red means go . . . home.

REPORTING THE (GOOD) NEWS

About two years after Jim and I had been married, we were blessed to conceive twins. We both wanted to have children together and had been heartbroken when my first pregnancy ended in a miscarriage. While carrying the twins, we were naturally worried at times and continually turned to the Lord for His perfect peace. The larger I grew with these two little lives inside me, the more I scaled back at work. I was still anchoring the morning news show for KETV but was excited about this new role as a mom I was about to begin.

I knew once the babies were born I would likely have to make a major career decision. Part of the issue involved my schedule. Going on air at 5:00 a.m. each day required me to get up at 2:00 a.m. in order to leave the house and get to work by 3:00 a.m. so I could prepare. This routine meant that I wouldn't be there most mornings when the kids woke up, nor would I get to spend much time with them because I was usually in bed by 5:00 or 6:00 p.m.

When I was about seven months pregnant, right before the arrival of our twins, I was enjoying a warm bath one evening when I suddenly heard God speaking to my heart. He told me to write down what He was telling me, so I jumped out of the tub—not easy to do when you're about to deliver twins!—grabbed a towel, and dashed into our bedroom in search of paper and pen. I began writing what God was telling me, writing as quickly as I could. It involved my future and what would become of my career.

Basically, God told me that after the twins came, about a year later I would be leaving my job, by my own choice. This caught me by surprise, and if anyone else but God had foretold this, I wouldn't have believed them. I loved being a broadcast journalist, and Jim and I had already discussed how we would manage once the twins were born. But I wasn't about to question God! I had trusted Him to bring me this far, so I knew He had something else in mind for me, which included being home for my new son and daughter.

Sure enough, about a year later, when Micah and Jemma turned one, I obeyed what God had told me to do and turned in my notice. While I was a little sad to end my career, at least for a while, I had no doubt it was what I needed to do. I had a strong sense that God had another direction in mind for me.

For about six or seven years, I enjoyed spending more time with the babies, supporting Jim, and being part of the leadership at Eagle's Nest. Then something amazing happened—once again, in the bathtub! I was enjoying a rare oasis of tranquility, just soaking in the peace of the warm water, when God spoke to my heart and told me that I was, again, about to give birth to twins. Confused, I sensed that, like before, He wanted me to get out of the tub and write down what He was telling me.

So I rushed into our bedroom in my robe, dripping water everywhere along the way, and began hurriedly writing down what He meant by these two new "babies" I was about to birth. First, He said that I would combine my past career experience with my passion for Him and launch a ministry TV show. My second baby involved something you already know about— writing this book!

And it's funny, too, because I quickly began assembling the team I would need to launch this new production when I felt prompted to call someone I had not talked to in a while: Roy Hamilton! Roy and I had stayed in touch over the years, but we had not talked since I had entered ministry full time. In fact, as I was dialing his number, I remembered that the last couple of times I had called and left a message, he had not called me back.

"Hey, Roy!" I said, leaving a voice mail. "It's Elictia. I'd love to catch up and get your advice about a new project I'm doing. Please give me a call at your convenience. I hope you're doing well! Bye, now."

My phone rang five minutes later, and Roy and I had a great chat. We caught up on each other's lives as he shared about his recent retirement from FOX as senior vice president of talent and development. Then, when I told him what I was doing and asked if he had any suggestions about someone to produce my new show, Roy said, "I could help you out!"

"Thank you so much, Roy," I said. "But there's no way I can afford someone as experienced as you. I need someone who—"

"Hey, don't worry about it," he said. "I would really love to do this and help you out."

We continued talking, and I couldn't believe that Roy was so excited about producing my new television show. True to his word, Roy became our executive producer and provided so much wisdom and experience as we started this new venture. In fact, we were in Santa Monica a few months later, not far from where we had that first conversation in his office more than fifteen years earlier. Roy was impressed by the content and message I now shared in front of the camera. No longer reporting the news, I now got to share the good news!

After we finished that shoot in California, Roy said, "You haven't changed a bit—still great in front of that camera and you have a special way of communicating the Lord's message to the world. Guess you had a bit of practice over the years."

"Thanks, Roy," I said, laughing. "I do my best and leave the rest up to God."

I was thrilled to have one of my greatest mentors around once again. And to hear him say he was proud of all that I had done and become, along with being impressed with my ability to communicate so well meant the absolute world to me.

Once again, when I was staring at a red-light moment face-to-face, the Lord jumped in. Roy surpassed all I could have imagined in terms of executive producing my show. There are very few people who can do what he does as far as putting together a good television show. I think I might have pinched myself when I left California later that week. Once again, I knew God had me exactly where I was supposed to be. Another red light turned green!

IF GOD IS FOR YOU

From the red carpet to the pulpit, I've remained willing to go where the Lord called me—and I've never looked back. My heart's cry is to make Him famous. As I've shared with you throughout these pages, God has been so good to me and so faithful to draw me closer to Him. No matter the circumstances of my life, I've been blessed to experience His love in so many different and wonderful ways—through Jim, our precious kids, our church family, our extended family, and close friends.

For most of my broadcasting career, I worked in a male-dominated field. But I always knew I had the greatest male who ever walked the face of the earth on my side. I had Jesus—and I still do! His mercies are new every morning, and I marvel at how He continues to bless me.

God cares for you just as much. No matter what you have done or haven't done, who you used to be, or where you come from, He will never give up on loving you and transforming you into the likeness of His Son. He is so great and so loving that we can't even begin to grasp how much He cares for us. In the Bible God tells us, "My thoughts are not your thoughts, neither are your ways my ways. . . . As the heavens are higher than the earth, so are my ways higher than your ways and my thoughts than your thoughts" (Isa. 55:8–9). In his epistle to the church at Rome, Paul also reminded us, "Who has known the mind of the Lord? Or who has been his counselor?" (Rom. 11:34).

Obviously, we cannot fully comprehend what it means to know God, to be loved by Him, and to be empowered by His Spirit. But He does reveal Himself to us when we seek Him. Even though He defies human description, our God is so great that He gives us images and metaphors to help us know Him and His character. He is like the wind and like fire. He is like the rain, like the lamb sacrificed by the high priest on the altar. He is revealed in the beauty of His creation and His incredible handiwork in nature.

God is in a class all by Himself!

And the power of His love in your life is also beyond compare. Are you willing to let Him in all the way? To follow Him in the midst of uncertainty, doubts, fears, and mistakes?

What would you do if you were absolutely confident that God was with you? Think about it. How would you respond in your current circumstances, right here and right now, if you were totally confident that God is for you?

With this assurance, perhaps in the process of walking out your dreams and living out your purpose, you would be a bit more confident. Perhaps you would respond to situations differently knowing, "If God be for me, who can be against me?" Knowing, "I'm more than a conqueror." Knowing, "I can do all things through Christ who strengthens me." Knowing, "The battle is His and not mine."

Knowing and understanding the loving character of God will allow you to rely on Him. You will gain a better understanding that it's not by might nor by power, but it's by God's Spirit that you will be successful in this life. You don't need to reinvent the wheel or take matters into your own hands to get ahead in life. You simply need to be attuned to the Holy Spirit dwelling within you and follow His gentle prompting as you seek God and obey His commandments.

My prayer for you as our journey together concludes is that you would never forget the infinite love of our most gracious God. He can do the impossible—way more than you can ever hope or imagine! So when you see the color red, when you face moments that seem too hard to bear, I hope you'll remember to redefine them as opportunities for God to work in your life. Redefining red transforms those moments of crisis into unexpected blessings.

Whether it's signaling danger or destruction, crisis or catastrophe, peril or pressure, redefining red means you can remain calm and trust in your Father to guide you and provide all you need. He is always with you, no matter what you face, and He will redeem even the hardest, most painful parts of your life if you will let Him.

Godspeed on your journey!

SHIFTING RED MOMENTS TO GREEN TRIUMPHS

GO DEEPER

How do you usually handle big changes in your life? When was the last time you experienced an unexpected big change?

What did it involve? Was it a move, a loss, a new beginning? Something else? How did God meet you in the midst of this change? What did you learn from embracing the opportunity to change?

GO FURTHER

Dear God,

Nothing compares to You! Thank You for loving me so much that You sent Your Son to die for me. I can't even comprehend what that means, but I want to spend the rest of my life discovering more of Your love and sharing it with everyone around me.

So much of life causes me to worry if I dwell on it and allow it to occupy my thoughts. Help me take such anxious thoughts captive to the power of Christ and to rest in the knowledge of Your sovereignty and goodness.

Whether I face terrible losses and unexpected trials or dangerous moments and painful betrayals, remind me of Your love and strength to keep me going. I love You, Lord, and I can't wait to see what You have in store for me next! In Jesus' name, amen.

ACKNOWLEDGMENTS

W hen the Lord planted the seed for *Redefining Red*, I thought, *Oh, my goodness, I have my work cut out for me. You want me to write a book, Lord?* The task seemed daunting and larger than life. However, I knew if He was prompting me, then He already saw the finished product, and that encouraged me to pick up my pen and start writing, which is what I did!

As I wrote, the Lord blessed me with so many people who crossed my path and helped cultivate the words until this book blossomed. Early in the process, friends like Karen Williams and Kevin Light provided crucial encouragement and editorial expertise. I'm also grateful to Dudley Delffs for his coaching, wordsmithing, and for introducing me to my publisher. Thank you, Dudley, you are the BEST!

I'm so thankful to have a publisher like Joel Kneedler at Emanate. His support, patience, and standard of excellence continue to mean so much to me. I also appreciate Janene MacIvor, my senior editor, who is absolutely brilliant at what she does. She has grown to be one of my favorite people in this process. Additionally, I'm thankful to everyone at Thomas Nelson for their incredible attention to detail and dedication to my labor of love. I feel so blessed to work with this amazing team.

A special thanks to my husband, my forever love and greatest support. Babe, for all the times I was writing in the car, stealing away to write for a few minutes on vacation, and up all hours of the night writing, thank you for your patience. You encouraged me as I wrote, every step of the way. You are truly the wind beneath my wings, my best half, and so much more. As I have said many times, when our Creator made you, He must have had me in His back pocket. That's just how perfect you are for me. I love you with all my heart and my extra (heart) chamber!

Thanks to my beautiful twins, Micah and Jemma, who continued to wonder if I would ever finish writing this book and when they would actually be able to see it, hold it, and if anyone would actually read it! Ha ha! You are Mom's greatest blessings and your patience through this process has not gone unnoticed! Muah!

I'm so grateful to my parents, Larry and Melanie, and two younger sisters, Joffrey and Tessa, who walked through many of the "red-light" moments I wrote about in this book. Dad and Mom, you have always been a source of encouragement during these challenging seasons in my life and for that I'm thankful. You truly watched me turn my red-light moments into green-light victories. Now, that's what I call family!

A ginormous shout-out to my prayer warrior team who helped birth this book in the Spirit. Miriam, Sis. Mitchell, Sis. Brunt and Becca you are amazing. We spent so much time in our prayer closets and face-to-face praying. Let's not forget laughing, crying, watching, and waiting as the Lord was busy doing the rest. We saw red lights truly become green lights right in front of our very eyes. I love you all deeply. Thank you . . . yes, thank you!

ACKNOWLEDGMENTS

Pastors Sam and Eva Rodriguez, thank you for always being willing to see green lights while dreaming with Jim and me. Your friendship means the world and we love you both dearly. We have and will continue to *redefine red* together for sure!

Kevin, Roy, Mitch, and the many others who have journeyed with me along the way—thank you! To those I have not mentioned, because I honestly would need another entire book, thank you for your support and love.

Finally, I could never have created this book without the support of my church family at Eagle's Nest Worship Center. I say it all the time: we have the best church in the world!

ABOUT THE
AUTHOR

Pastor Elictia Hart and her husband Pastor James Hart are the leaders of Eagle's Nest Worship Center in Omaha, Nebraska, one of the largest, most diverse congregations in the region. For almost twenty years this Seattle native traveled the globe as a television journalist working for CNBC, *Entertainment Tonight*, ESPN, and various network affiliates. Today Pastor Elictia combines her former career with her current passion by preaching God's perfect truth on her television show *Live Your Journey*, which airs on the worldwide networks TBN Salsa and the Faith Broadcasting Network (FBN). Every year, in addition to her domestic speaking schedule, Elictia accepts multiple invitations to preach in places such as Brazil, Burkina Faso, the Caribbean, Hong Kong, Latvia, New Zealand, South Africa, and Zimbabwe. She is the mother of twins Micah and Jemma and lives in Nebraska.